Wiccan Philosophy and Ethics

Wiccan Wisdom: Exploring the Philosophy and Ethics of the Craft

Olivia Hartmann

Table of Contents

INTRODUCTION

In the mystical realms of the Craft, where the ancient meets the modern and the sacred embraces the mundane, lies a spiritual path known as Wicca. Rooted in nature, the cycles of the seasons, and the reverence for both the divine feminine and masculine, Wicca is a vibrant and evolving tradition that has captivated the hearts as well as minds of countless seekers around the world. It is a path of profound wisdom, enchanting rituals, and a unique ethical framework that guides the lives of its practitioners.

Welcome to "Wiccan Philosophy and Ethics: Wiccan Wisdom - Exploring the Philosophy and Ethics of the Craft." Within these pages, we embark on a journey into the heart and soul of Wicca, uncovering the deep philosophical foundations and ethical principles that underpin this enchanting spiritual practice. Whether you are a seasoned Wiccan seeking a deeper understanding of your tradition or a curious soul eager to explore the mysteries of Wicca for the first time, this book is your key to unlocking the profound wisdom that Wicca has to offer.

Wicca is often misunderstood and mischaracterized, shrouded in stereotypes and misconceptions. This book aims to demystify Wicca and provide a comprehensive and insightful exploration of its philosophy and ethics. We will delve into the core beliefs that shape Wiccan thought, such as the Wiccan Rede, the Threefold Law, and the worship of the Goddess and God. We will explore the sacred Wheel of the Year and the profound significance of its eight Sabbats, as well as the intricate art of Wiccan ritual and magick.

Wicca is not just a spiritual path; it's a way of life. It offers a unique ethical framework that emphasizes harmony, responsibility, and the preservation of the natural world. We will dive into the intricacies of Wiccan ethics and morality, discussing how these principles guide decision-making and contribute to personal growth and transformation.

As we navigate this journey together, you will discover that Wicca is not only a source of spiritual enlightenment but also a wellspring of practical wisdom that can enrich every aspect of your life. So, let us embark on this voyage of discovery, and may the wisdom of Wicca illuminate your path, offering insights, inspiration, and a deeper connection to the Craft.

CHAPTER I

Understanding Wicca

Brief History of Wicca

Wicca, a modern pagan, witchcraft-based religion, has a history that spans just a few short decades, yet it draws inspiration from centuries of magical and mystical traditions. Born in the mid-20th century, Wicca emerged as a reaction to the prevailing religious and social norms of the time. To understand the history of Wicca, one must explore its key figures, the influences that shaped it, and its evolution into the diverse and vibrant movement it is today.

The roots of Wicca can be traced back to the British occultist Gerald Gardner, often referred to as the "Father of Wicca." In the 1950s, Gardner claimed to have been initiated into a surviving witchcraft tradition by a woman named Dorothy Clutterbuck. Gardner's publication of "Witchcraft Today" in 1954 and "The Meaning of Witchcraft" in 1959 introduced Wicca to the world. These books presented a blend of ceremonial magic, folklore, and nature-based spirituality that would become the cornerstone of modern Wicca.

However, Gardner did not work in isolation. He was influenced by various sources, including the writings of Margaret Murray, an archaeologist and folklorist who proposed the theory of an ancient witch-cult surviving through the ages. While Murray's theory has been widely discredited by historians, it played a role in shaping the romanticized image of witchcraft that influenced Gardner and later Wiccan practitioners.

Another significant figure in the early history of Wicca is Doreen Valiente, often called the "Mother of Modern Witchcraft." Valiente collaborated with Gardner, helping to refine and expand upon the rituals and liturgy of Wicca. Her poetic contributions to the religion, such as the Charge of the Goddess, continue to be revered by Wiccans today.

The 1960s and 1970s saw the spread of Wicca beyond British shores. Raymond Buckland, an Englishman who had been initiated into Gardnerian Wicca, brought the tradition to the United States and initiated the first American coven in 1963. His book, "Witchcraft Today," served as a primer for many early American Wiccans. In addition to Gardnerian Wicca, other Wiccan traditions, such as Alexandrian and Dianic, emerged during this period, each with its own variations in practice and belief.

The 1970s also witnessed the rise of feminist spirituality and the inclusion of women's empowerment within the framework of Wicca. The Dianic tradition, founded by Zsuzsanna Budapest, placed a strong emphasis on the Goddess and the celebration of female divinity. This shift brought greater diversity to Wicca, as practitioners explored the intersections of feminism, environmentalism, and spirituality.

The 1980s and 1990s marked a period of growth for Wicca, with more books, websites, and resources becoming available to those interested in the religion. This accessibility led to a proliferation of solitary practitioners and the creation of new eclectic and solitary traditions. Wicca's emphasis on personal experience and self-discovery allowed it to adapt to the needs and beliefs of individual practitioners.

Wicca's history is not without controversy and criticism. Skeptics and scholars have questioned the validity of its claims to ancient origins, as there is little historical evidence to support the existence of a continuous witchcraft tradition dating back centuries. Additionally, some early Wiccan leaders have been accused of embellishing or fabricating their stories to lend credibility to the religion.

In recent years, Wicca has continued to evolve. It has embraced LGBTQ+ inclusivity, environmental activism, and social justice causes. Many modern Wiccans prioritize eco-spirituality, emphasizing a profound connection with nature and a responsibility to protect the environment.

In conclusion, Wicca's history is a relatively short but complex narrative of innovation, adaptation, and the blending of diverse influences. From the visionary Gerald Gardner and the poetic Doreen Valiente to the feminist and eclectic branches of the religion, Wicca has continuously evolved to meet the spiritual needs of its practitioners. Its legacy endures as a testament to the human desire for connection with the sacred, the mystical, and the natural world.

The Nature of Wiccan Spirituality

Wiccan spirituality is a tapestry woven from threads of ancient wisdom, reverence for nature, and a deep connection to the divine. Rooted in the belief that the sacred is immanent in the world around us, Wicca offers a unique and vibrant approach to spirituality that has resonated with countless individuals seeking a meaningful connection with the mysteries of existence. To understand the nature of Wiccan spirituality, one must explore its core beliefs, practices, and the profound connection it fosters between practitioners and the natural world.

At the heart of Wiccan spirituality lies a profound reverence for nature and the cycles of the natural world. Wiccans view the Earth as a living, sacred entity deserving of respect and protection. This perspective is embodied in the Wiccan Rede, a moral guideline that encapsulates the central tenet of Wiccan ethics: "An it harm none, do what ye will." This simple yet profound principle emphasizes the importance of living in harmony with all living beings and the environment. It reflects the belief that every action has consequences and that ethical considerations should guide one's choices.

Central to Wiccan spirituality is the veneration of the Goddess and God, often represented as the divine feminine and masculine principles. Wicca embraces a polytheistic or pantheistic worldview, acknowledging the presence of many deities within the natural world. The Goddess is often associated with the cycles of the moon, the nurturing qualities of the Earth, and the mysteries of birth, life, death, and rebirth. The God embodies the vitality of the sun, the wildness of the forest, and the cycles of growth and decay. Together, they form a sacred duality that reflects the interplay of opposites in the cosmos.

Wiccan spirituality also places great importance on the practice of magick, spelled with a "k" to distinguish it from stage magic. Magick in Wicca is not about supernatural feats but rather the art of harnessing natural energies and intentions to create change in one's life and surroundings. Rituals and spells are employed as tools to focus intention, attune with the divine, and manifest desired outcomes. These practices are often performed within a sacred circle, a symbolic boundary that separates the mundane from the sacred and provides a protected space for ritual work.

The Wheel of the Year, a sacred calendar of festivals and sabbats, forms another essential aspect of Wiccan spirituality. These eight seasonal celebrations mark key points in the agricultural and astronomical calendar, aligning with the solstices, equinoxes, and other significant natural events. Each sabbat is an opportunity for Wiccans to connect with the changing rhythms of the

Earth, honor the deities, and participate in rituals that reflect the themes of the season, such as growth, harvest, or rebirth.

Wiccan spirituality is characterized by its inclusivity and flexibility. Unlike some religious traditions with rigid dogmas, Wicca encourages personal exploration and interpretation. Many Wiccans consider themselves eclectic, drawing from a variety of sources and traditions to create a spiritual practice that resonates with their individual beliefs and experiences. This eclecticism is not seen as a weakness but rather as a strength, allowing for spiritual growth and adaptation to the changing demands of practitioners.

The practice of Wicca is often solitary, with individuals crafting their own rituals and spells. However, it can also be communal, with covens or circles coming together to celebrate the sabbats and share in the spiritual journey. Covens are groups of Wiccans who work closely together, often guided by a High Priestess and High Priest, and follow specific traditions or lineages. These covens provide a sense of community, support, and shared knowledge.

Wiccan spirituality is not limited to the confines of rituals and festivals; it extends into everyday life. Wiccans seek to integrate their spiritual beliefs into their daily routines, fostering mindfulness, gratitude, and a sense of responsibility toward the Earth and all its inhabitants. This holistic approach to spirituality underscores the idea that Wicca is not just a religion but a way of life.

In conclusion, the nature of Wiccan spirituality is a harmonious blend of reverence for nature, devotion to the Goddess and God, the practice of magick, and the celebration of the Wheel of the Year. It is a spiritual path that honors the interconnectedness of all living things and seeks to cultivate a deep sense of responsibility and stewardship for the Earth. Wicca's flexibility and inclusivity allow individuals to craft a unique and deeply personal spiritual practice that resonates with their own beliefs and experiences. Whether practiced in solitude or within a coven, Wicca offers a profound and meaningful way to connect with the divine and the natural world.

CHAPTER II

The Basics of Wiccan Beliefs

The Wiccan Rede

The Wiccan Rede, a concise and enigmatic statement, holds a central place in the ethical framework of Wiccan spirituality. It encapsulates the fundamental principle of "An it harm none, do what ye will," and serves as a guiding light for modern witches and practitioners of Wicca. To truly have an understanding of the depth and significance of the Wiccan Rede, one must delve into its origins, its interpretations, and its profound impact on the practice of Wicca as a whole.

The Wiccan Rede, often pronounced as "reed," can be traced back to the mid-20th century, during the formative years of Wicca as a recognized spiritual tradition. It is closely associated with Gerald Gardner, one of the key figures in the early history of Wicca. Gardner, considered by many as the "Father of Wicca," introduced the Rede to the wider world in his books, "Witchcraft Today" (1954) and "The Meaning of Witchcraft" (1959). However, the exact origin of the Rede is shrouded in mystery, and it is unclear whether Gardner himself coined the phrase or inherited it from older sources.

The Rede's core message is deceptively simple: "An it harm none, do what ye will." At first glance, it appears to grant practitioners carte blanche to pursue their desires without ethical restraint. However, a deeper examination reveals the profound moral philosophy embedded within these words. The phrase "an it harm none" serves as a critical qualifier, placing a crucial condition on the pursuit of one's will. It emphasizes the significance of considering the potential harm or consequences of one's actions before proceeding.

This ethical guideline encourages practitioners to live their lives in harmony with the world around them, recognizing that their actions have an impact not only on themselves but also on others and the environment. It reflects the interconnectedness of all things, a central tenet of Wiccan spirituality. By following the Rede, Wiccans strive to avoid causing harm, whether physical, emotional, or spiritual, to any living being, including themselves.

Interpreting the Rede is not always straightforward, and discussions within the Wiccan community often revolve around its nuances. Some argue that the Rede promotes a form of ethical relativism, allowing individuals to determine what constitutes harm based on their own judgment. Others believe it calls for a careful consideration of the consequences of one's actions and decisions, acknowledging that some actions may be necessary despite potential harm, as long as they are for the greater good and within the bounds of responsibility.

The Rede's flexibility is both its strength and its challenge. While it provides a broad ethical framework, it also leaves room for interpretation, leading to a diversity of perspectives within the Wiccan community. Some Wiccans adhere strictly to the Rede's literal interpretation, while others view it as a guiding principle that requires thoughtful consideration and adaptation to specific situations.

One common interpretation of the Rede emphasizes the importance of personal responsibility. Practitioners are encouraged to weigh the potential consequences of their actions carefully and make choices that align with the highest ethical standards. This interpretation recognizes that life is complex, and ethical dilemmas can arise in various forms. It calls for a deep awareness of one's intentions and a commitment to minimizing harm whenever possible.

The Rede also extends beyond individual ethics to address the broader Wiccan community and its interactions with the world. Many Wiccans believe that the Rede underscores their responsibility to preserve and also care for the Earth, promoting environmental stewardship as an integral aspect of their spirituality. This ecological perspective aligns with the recognition of the Earth as sacred in Wiccan belief, emphasizing the interconnectedness of all life.

The Wiccan Rede's influence extends far beyond the realm of ethics; it shapes the rituals, spells, and magickal practices of modern witches. The Rede's emphasis on harmlessness and responsibility guides the intentions behind magickal workings. Wiccans believe that any magickal act must be aligned with the Rede, ensuring that it does not harm others or interfere with their free will. This principle has led to the development of ethical guidelines for spellwork, such as not performing love spells that infringe upon another's autonomy.

The Rede also plays a significant role in the celebration of the Wiccan Wheel of the Year, the eight sabbats that mark the changing seasons and cycles of the natural world. Each sabbat is an opportunity for reflection on the Rede's ethical principles and a reminder of the interconnectedness of all life.

In conclusion, the Wiccan Rede stands as a foundational ethical guideline in the practice of modern Wicca. Its simple yet profound message, "An it harm none, do what ye will," encapsulates the essence of Wiccan spirituality, emphasizing harmlessness, responsibility, and the interconnectedness of all life. While interpretations of the Rede may vary, its core principles of ethical consideration and reverence for the natural world continue to guide the path of modern witches and provide a moral compass for those who seek to live in harmony with the sacred web of existence.

The Threefold Law

Within the rich tapestry of Wiccan spirituality and ethics, the Threefold Law stands as a key principle, often expressed as "Whatever you send out into the world, be it positive or negative, shall return to you threefold." This concept, reminiscent of the universal law of karma, is a central tenet of Wiccan morality and guides the actions and intentions of practitioners. To understand the Threefold Law, one must delve into its origins, interpretations, and the profound impact it has on the practice of Wicca.

The Threefold Law, also known as the Law of Return or the Rule of Three, is closely associated with the modern witchcraft movement and contemporary Wicca. While it is commonly referenced in Wiccan literature, its precise origins remain somewhat elusive. Some attribute the law to the influential Wiccan figure Gerald Gardner, while others believe it emerged as part of the broader neo-pagan and witchcraft revival in the mid-20th century. Regardless of its exact origins, the Threefold Law has become a fundamental component of Wiccan ethics and spirituality.

At its core, the Threefold Law is a statement of cause and effect, reflecting the belief that one's actions and intentions reverberate through the cosmos and return to the individual, magnified threefold. It serves as a moral compass, encouraging practitioners to consider the consequences of their actions and the energy they release into the world. This concept mirrors the idea of karma in various Eastern spiritual traditions, where one's deeds, whether good or bad, have repercussions that affect their future experiences.

Interpreting the Threefold Law can be both straightforward and complex. On the surface, it appears to advocate a form of cosmic justice, wherein positive actions yield positive outcomes, and negative actions result in negative consequences. However, delving deeper reveals a more nuanced understanding. The law emphasizes that energy is neither created nor destroyed but merely transformed. In this context, the "return" of one's actions is not necessarily punitive but rather a reflection of the interconnectedness of all life.

Wiccans often view the Threefold Law as a reminder of personal responsibility and ethical consideration. It encourages practitioners to act with mindfulness, ensuring that their intentions align with harmlessness and the greater good. For example, if a Wiccan were to perform a spell or ritual with the intention of causing harm to another, they would anticipate that this negative energy would eventually return to them, potentially with greater intensity. This understanding dissuades practitioners from engaging in harmful or malevolent actions.

However, interpreting the Threefold Law can be challenging, as it raises questions about intention versus outcome. Some practitioners argue that it is not the mere act of causing harm but the intent behind the action that determines the karmic consequences. In this view, if an action with negative consequences was performed with good intentions, the return of energy may be less severe or may even yield positive outcomes. This perspective highlights the importance of discerning one's motives and being aware of the ethical nuances of each situation.

Critics of the Threefold Law argue that it oversimplifies the complex nature of ethical decision-making and the consequences of actions. They suggest that life is rarely so binary, and the law's emphasis on a strict threefold return can lead to a fear-based approach to spirituality.

Some practitioners may become overly cautious or hesitant to take risks, fearing potential negative repercussions. Additionally, the law's deterministic nature implies a lack of free will, as individuals are bound to receive specific outcomes based solely on their actions.

Despite these criticisms, the Threefold Law remains a foundational principle for many Wiccans and continues to influence their approach to magick, ritual, and daily life. It fosters an awareness of the interconnectedness of all living beings and encourages practitioners to strive for harmlessness and ethical behavior. It also serves as a cautionary reminder to approach the practice of magick with mindfulness and responsibility, as the energy one releases into the world can have far-reaching consequences.

In practice, the Threefold Law often guides the intentions behind spells and rituals. Wiccans seek to align their magickal workings with the principles of harmlessness and the greater good, understanding that the energy they release will eventually return to them. This approach to magick emphasizes the importance of ethical considerations in spellcasting and reinforces the idea that magick is a tool for personal and spiritual growth rather than a means to manipulate others or the natural world.

The Threefold Law also extends to broader ethical considerations, such as environmental stewardship and social responsibility. Many Wiccans believe that the law underscores their duty to preserve as well as care for the Earth, recognizing that harm to the environment can result in negative consequences for all living beings, including themselves. This ecological perspective aligns with the reverence for nature that is central to Wiccan spirituality.

In conclusion, the Threefold Law stands as a cornerstone of Wiccan ethics and spirituality, reflecting the belief that one's actions and intentions have repercussions that return to them, magnified threefold. While interpretations of the law may vary, its core principles of personal responsibility, harmlessness, and the interconnectedness of all life continue to shape the moral compass of modern witches. Whether viewed as a cosmic justice system or a reminder of ethical considerations, the Threefold Law underscores the importance of mindfulness and responsibility in the practice of Wicca, encouraging practitioners to navigate their spiritual journey with care and integrity.

The Concept of Deity in Wicca

Central to Wicca, a modern pagan, witchcraft-based religion, is the concept of deity. Wiccans embrace a unique and multifaceted understanding of the divine, characterized by the veneration of both the Goddess and the God. This dualistic approach to the divine reflects a profound connection to the cycles of nature and the rhythms of life and death. To comprehend the concept of deity in Wicca, one must explore the symbolism, mythology, and significance of the Goddess and God, as well as their role in the spirituality and practice of Wiccans.

The Goddess and the God in Wicca represent the divine feminine and masculine principles, respectively. They are often personified through various names and archetypes, reflecting their roles in the natural world and the cycles of existence. The Goddess is commonly associated with the phases of the moon, embodying the Maiden, Mother, and Crone aspects. The Maiden represents youth, innocence, and new beginnings, the Mother embodies nurturing, fertility, and abundance, while the Crone symbolizes wisdom, transformation, and the waning moon. The God, on the other hand, is associated with the cycles of the sun, reflecting birth, life, death, and rebirth. He is often represented as the Horned God, a figure linked to the wild and untamed aspects of nature.

The veneration of the Goddess and God in Wicca reflects a harmonious balance of opposites. Their duality mirrors the interconnectedness of life and death, light and darkness, and the cyclical nature of existence. This dualistic approach to the divine emphasizes the idea that both feminine and masculine energies are necessary for creation, balance, and the continuation of life. It encourages practitioners to recognize and honor the sacredness of all aspects of existence, including those often associated with change and transformation.

The veneration of the Goddess and God is not limited to ritual and symbolism; it extends to the celebration of the Wiccan Wheel of the Year, a sacred calendar consisting of eight sabbats that mark the changing seasons and natural cycles. Each sabbat is an opportunity for Wiccans to connect with the energies of the Goddess and God and to reflect on the mysteries of life, death, and rebirth. For example, the holiday of Beltane, celebrated in May, honors the union of the God and Goddess, symbolizing the fertile energy of spring. Samhain, celebrated in October, marks the time when the God descends into the underworld, reflecting the waning energy of the sun and the approach of winter.

The concept of deity in Wicca also embraces a pantheistic or polytheistic worldview. While Wiccans may work with specific deities and pantheons from various mythologies, they often view these deities as facets or expressions of the broader divine energy. This perspective allows for a flexible and eclectic approach to deity, where practitioners may choose to work with deities that resonate with their personal beliefs and experiences. It also reflects the idea that the divine is immanent in the natural world, and every aspect of nature can be a source of inspiration and reverence.

Wiccan rituals and magickal practices frequently involve the invocation and worship of the Goddess and God. The casting of the sacred circle, a fundamental component of Wiccan ritual, is often accompanied by calling upon the divine energies of the Goddess and God to bless and protect the ritual space. These invocations serve as a means of connecting with the divine and seeking guidance, inspiration, and empowerment in magickal workings.

The use of symbols, such as the pentacle, the moon, and the sun, also plays a significant role in the veneration of the Goddess and God. These symbols serve as representations of the divine energies and are integrated into rituals, spells, and magickal tools. For example, the pentacle, a five-pointed star enclosed in a circle, is often used to symbolize the five elements and the divine harmony of the universe. The moon, representing the Goddess, is associated with intuition, receptivity, and the mysteries of the subconscious. The sun, representing the God, symbolizes strength, vitality, and the conscious mind.

Wiccan rituals and spellwork often incorporate the symbolism of the Goddess and God to align with specific intentions and energies. For example, a love spell may invoke the energies of the Goddess of love and the God of passion to enhance the spell's effectiveness. Similarly, a healing ritual may call upon the nurturing aspects of the Mother Goddess and the vitality of the Sun God to promote health and well-being.

The concept of deity in Wicca is not limited to a distant and transcendent divine being but emphasizes the immanence of the divine in the natural world and within each individual. This understanding encourages practitioners to recognize their own divine potential and to connect with the divine energies within themselves. Wicca teaches that the divine resides in all living beings, and each person has the capacity to access and channel divine energies in their spiritual practice and daily life.

In conclusion, the concept of deity in Wicca is a profound and multifaceted understanding of the divine, characterized by the veneration of the Goddess and the God. This dualistic approach reflects the interconnectedness of all life, the cycles of nature, and the balance of opposites. The Goddess and God are honored through symbolism, mythology, and ritual, and their energies are invoked in magickal practices. The concept of deity in Wicca also emphasizes a pantheistic or polytheistic worldview, allowing for a diverse and eclectic approach to working with deities. Ultimately, the understanding of deity in Wicca encourages practitioners to recognize the divine within themselves and to foster a deep connection with the sacred energies of the natural world.

The Elements and Directions

The elements and directions are integral components of Wiccan spirituality and magickal practice, providing a framework for understanding the natural world, the divine energies, and the interconnectedness of all life. In Wicca, the elements—Earth, Air, Fire, Water, and Spirit— are associated with specific qualities, energies, and correspondences, while the directions—North, East, South, West, and Center—provide a symbolic and spiritual orientation. To comprehend the significance of the elements and directions in Wicca, one must explore their symbolism, their role in ritual and spellwork, and their connection to the broader spiritual worldview of Wiccans.

The five elements—Earth, Air, Fire, Water, and Spirit— serve as foundational building blocks of the natural world and are revered as sacred forces in Wicca. Each element embodies specific qualities and energies that resonate with different aspects of existence. Earth represents stability, fertility, and the physical realm. It is associated with the north, the color green or brown, and the pentacle symbol. Air embodies intellect, communication, and the realm of thought. It is associated with the east, the color yellow or white, and the athame, or ritual knife. Fire symbolizes passion, transformation, and the spark of inspiration. It is associated with the south, the color red or orange, and the wand or staff. Water signifies emotion, intuition, and the realm of feelings. It is associated with the west, the color blue or silver, and the chalice or cup. Spirit, often referred to as the quintessence or ether, represents the divine, the sacred, and the interconnectedness of all life.

In Wiccan rituals and spellwork, the elements are called upon and invoked to lend their energies and attributes to the working. This process, known as "casting a circle" or "calling the quarters," involves consecrating and creating a sacred space by acknowledging the presence and influence of each element and direction. Wiccans often start in the east, invoking the element of Air, which represents new beginnings, clarity, and the power of thought. Moving clockwise, they proceed to the south, invoking Fire, symbolizing transformation, creativity, and the courage to act. Next, they invoke Water in the west, representing emotions, intuition, and the flow of life. Finally, they call upon Earth in the north, symbolizing stability, abundance, and grounding.

The center, known as the "center of the circle" or the "heart of the ritual," represents the fifth element, Spirit. It is often associated with the divine, the source of all energy, and the interconnectedness of all life. The center is where the practitioner stands or sits during the ritual, symbolizing their role as a bridge between the physical and the spiritual realms. It is a place of balance, reflection, and alignment with the sacred energies of the elements.

The directions in Wicca, often referred to as the "quarters" or "cardinal points," provide a symbolic orientation and alignment with the energies of the elements. Each direction is associated with specific correspondences and qualities. North, representing Earth, embodies qualities of stability, endurance, and the material world. It is associated with the color green or brown, the element of Earth, and the pentacle symbol. East, representing Air, symbolizes intellect, communication, and the realm of thought. It is associated with the color yellow or white, the element of Air, and the athame. South, representing Fire, signifies passion, transformation, and the spark of inspiration. It is associated with the color red or orange, the element of Fire, and the wand or staff. West, representing Water, embodies emotion, intuition, and the realm of feelings. It is associated with the color blue or silver, the element of Water, and the chalice or cup.

The directions serve as a spiritual compass, helping Wiccans attune to the energies of the elements and their corresponding qualities. In ritual and spellwork, practitioners often face or acknowledge the specific directions associated with their intentions. For example, if one is performing a spell for healing or emotional balance, they may turn to the west to connect with the energies of Water and the qualities associated with that direction.

The elements and directions are not only integral to ritual and spellwork but also play a significant role in Wiccan cosmology and worldview. They represent the interconnectedness of all life and the sacredness of the natural world. Wiccans view the elements as divine forces present in every aspect of existence, from the physical to the spiritual. This perspective aligns with the belief that nature is a source of inspiration, wisdom, and spiritual insight.

The concept of the elements and directions in Wicca is not limited to ritual and magickal practice; it extends to everyday life. Wiccans seek to align their actions and intentions with the qualities and energies of the elements, fostering a more profound connection to the natural world and a sense of balance and harmony. For example, they may draw upon the stability of Earth when seeking financial abundance or grounding, or they may invoke the clarity of Air when making decisions or seeking knowledge.

In conclusion, the elements and directions in Wicca are profound and multifaceted symbols that embody the qualities and energies of the natural world. They serve as a framework for understanding the interconnectedness of all life and provide a spiritual orientation in ritual and spellwork. The elements represent Earth, Air, Fire, Water, and Spirit, each with its unique attributes, correspondences, and symbolism. The directions—North, East, South, West, and Center—align with the elements and offer a symbolic compass for attuning to the energies of the natural world. The concept of the elements and directions in Wicca underscores the sacredness of nature, the interconnectedness of all life, and the importance of mindfulness and balance in both spiritual practice and daily life.

CHAPTER III

Wiccan Ethics

The Importance of Ethics in Wicca

Ethics form an integral and sacred aspect of Wiccan spirituality, serving as a moral compass that guides the actions, intentions, and interactions of practitioners. While Wicca is a diverse and eclectic belief system, it shares a fundamental ethical principle encapsulated in the Wiccan Rede: "An it harm none, do what ye will." This foundational maxim emphasizes harmlessness, personal responsibility, and the interconnectedness of all life. To truly grasp the importance of ethics in Wicca, one must delve into the origins of the Wiccan Rede, its interpretations, and its profound influence on the practice of modern witchcraft.

The Wiccan Rede, often pronounced as "reed," is a concise and enigmatic statement that embodies the central ethical tenet of Wicca. While its origins are somewhat mysterious, it is closely associated with Gerald Gardner, a prominent figure in the early history of Wicca. Gardner introduced the Rede to a wider audience through his books, "Witchcraft Today" (1954) and "The Meaning of Witchcraft" (1959). However, the Rede's roots likely extend further back into the folkloric and witchcraft traditions of Britain, reflecting a broader ethos of harmlessness and personal responsibility.

The central message of the Rede is deceptively simple: "An it harm none, do what ye will." At first glance, it appears to grant practitioners the freedom to pursue their desires and will without ethical restraint. However, a closer examination reveals a profound moral philosophy embedded within these words. The phrase "an it harm none" serves as a critical qualifier, placing a crucial condition on the pursuit of one's will. It emphasizes the importance of taking into account the potential harm or consequences of one's actions before proceeding.

This ethical guideline encourages practitioners to live their lives in harmony with the world around them, recognizing that their actions have an impact not only on themselves but also on others and the environment. It reflects the belief that every action has consequences and that ethical considerations should guide one's choices. The Rede calls for a deep awareness of the potential harm caused by one's actions and urges practitioners to choose paths that minimize or avoid harm altogether.

Interpreting the Rede is not always straightforward, and discussions within the Wiccan community often revolve around its nuances. Some argue that the Rede promotes a form of ethical relativism, allowing individuals to determine what constitutes harm based on their own judgment. Others believe it calls for a careful consideration of the consequences of one's actions and decisions, acknowledging that some actions may be necessary despite potential harm, as long as they are for the greater good and within the bounds of responsibility. The flexibility of the Rede is both its strength and its challenge. While it provides a broad ethical framework, it also leaves room for interpretation, leading to a diversity of perspectives within the Wiccan community. Some Wiccans adhere strictly to the Rede's literal interpretation, while others view it as a guiding principle that requires thoughtful consideration and adaptation to specific situations.

One common interpretation of the Rede emphasizes the importance of personal responsibility. Practitioners are encouraged to weigh the potential consequences of their actions carefully and make choices that align with the highest ethical standards. This interpretation recognizes that life is complex, and ethical dilemmas can arise in various forms. It calls for a deep awareness of one's intentions and a commitment to minimizing harm whenever possible.

The Rede also extends beyond individual ethics to address the broader Wiccan community and its interactions with the world. Many Wiccans believe that the Rede underscores their responsibility to protect as well as care for the Earth, promoting environmental stewardship as an integral aspect of their spirituality. This ecological perspective aligns with the recognition of the Earth as sacred in Wiccan belief, emphasizing the interconnectedness of all life.

The importance of ethics in Wicca is not confined to the confines of ritual and spellwork; it extends to everyday life. Wiccans seek to integrate their spiritual beliefs into their daily routines, fostering mindfulness, gratitude, and a sense of responsibility toward the Earth and all its inhabitants. This holistic approach to spirituality underscores the idea that Wicca is not just a religion but a way of life.

In the realm of ritual and magick, the Rede plays a significant role in guiding practitioners' intentions and actions. Wiccans believe that any magickal act must be aligned with the Rede, ensuring that it does not harm others or interfere with their free will. This principle has led to the development of ethical guidelines for spellwork, such as not performing love spells that infringe upon another's autonomy. The Rede reminds practitioners that their intentions and actions in the realm of magick carry ethical consequences and that personal responsibility is paramount.

Critics of the Rede argue that it oversimplifies the complex nature of ethical decision-making and the consequences of actions. They suggest that life is rarely so binary, and the Rede's emphasis on a strict threefold return can lead to a fear-based approach to spirituality. Some practitioners may become overly cautious or hesitant to take risks, fearing potential negative repercussions. Additionally, the Rede's deterministic nature implies a lack of free will, as individuals are bound to receive specific outcomes based solely on their actions.

Despite these criticisms, the Rede remains a foundational principle for many Wiccans and continues to influence their approach to magick, ritual, and daily life. It fosters an awareness of the interconnectedness of all living beings and encourages practitioners to strive for harmlessness and ethical behavior. It also serves as a cautionary reminder to approach the practice of magick with mindfulness and responsibility, as the energy one releases into the world can have far-reaching consequences.

In conclusion, the importance of ethics in Wicca cannot be overstated. The Wiccan Rede, encapsulating the central ethical tenet of the religion, emphasizes harmlessness, personal responsibility, and the interconnectedness of all life. It acts as an ethical compass that guides the actions, intentions, and choices of practitioners in ritual, spellwork, and daily life. While interpretations of the Rede may vary, its core principles of ethical consideration and reverence for the natural world continue to shape the moral compass of modern witches. Whether viewed as a cosmic justice system or a reminder of ethical considerations, the Rede underscores the importance of mindfulness and responsibility in the practice of Wicca, encouraging practitioners to navigate their spiritual journey with care and integrity.

Harm None: The Ethical Foundation

At the heart of Wicca, a modern pagan, witchcraft-based religion, lies a profound ethical principle often encapsulated in the Wiccan Rede: "An it harm none, do what ye will." This concise yet enigmatic statement serves as the ethical foundation of Wicca, guiding the actions, intentions, and interactions of practitioners. It is a principle of harmlessness, personal responsibility, and respect for the interconnectedness of all life. To truly appreciate the significance of "Harm None" in Wicca, one must explore its origins, interpretations, and its profound influence on the practice of modern witchcraft.

The Wiccan Rede, often pronounced as "reed," is a central ethical tenet within Wicca. While its precise origins remain somewhat mysterious, it is closely associated with Gerald Gardner, a prominent figure in the early history of Wicca. Gardner introduced the Rede to a wider audience through his books, "Witchcraft Today" (1954) and "The Meaning of Witchcraft" (1959). However, the Rede's roots likely extend further back into the folkloric and witchcraft traditions of Britain, reflecting a broader ethos of harmlessness and personal responsibility.

The central message of the Rede is deceptively simple: "An it harm none, do what ye will." On the surface, it may appear to grant practitioners the freedom to pursue their desires and will without ethical restraint. However, a closer examination reveals a profound moral philosophy embedded within these words. The phrase "an it harm none" serves as a critical qualifier, placing a crucial condition on the pursuit of one's will. It emphasizes the importance of taking into account the potential harm or consequences of one's actions before proceeding.

This ethical guideline encourages practitioners to live their lives in harmony with the world around them, recognizing that their actions have an impact not only on themselves but also on others and the environment. It reflects the belief that every action has consequences and that ethical considerations should guide one's choices. The Rede calls for a deep awareness of the potential harm caused by one's actions and urges practitioners to choose paths that minimize or avoid harm altogether.

Interpreting the Rede is not always straightforward, and discussions within the Wiccan community often revolve around its nuances. Some argue that the Rede promotes a form of ethical relativism, allowing individuals to determine what constitutes harm based on their own judgment. Others believe it calls for a careful consideration of the consequences of one's actions and decisions, acknowledging that some actions may be necessary despite potential harm, as long as they are for the greater good and within the bounds of responsibility. The flexibility of the Rede is both its strength and its challenge. While it provides a broad ethical framework, it also leaves room for interpretation, leading to a diversity of perspectives within the Wiccan community. Some Wiccans adhere strictly to the Rede's literal interpretation, while others view it as a guiding principle that requires thoughtful consideration and adaptation to specific situations.

One common interpretation of the Rede emphasizes the importance of personal responsibility. Practitioners are encouraged to weigh the potential consequences of their actions carefully and make choices that align with the highest ethical standards. This interpretation recognizes that life is complex, and ethical dilemmas can arise in various forms. It calls for a deep awareness of one's intentions and a commitment to minimizing harm whenever possible.

The Rede also extends beyond individual ethics to address the broader Wiccan community and its interactions with the world. Many Wiccans believe that the Rede underscores their responsibility to protect as well as care for the Earth, promoting environmental stewardship as an integral aspect of their spirituality. This ecological perspective aligns with the recognition of the Earth as sacred in Wiccan belief, emphasizing the interconnectedness of all life.

The importance of "Harm None" in Wicca is not confined to the confines of ritual and spellwork; it extends to everyday life. Wiccans seek to integrate their spiritual beliefs into their daily routines, fostering mindfulness, gratitude, and a sense of responsibility toward the Earth and all its inhabitants. This holistic approach to spirituality underscores the idea that Wicca is not just a religion but a way of life.

In the realm of ritual and magick, the Rede plays a significant role in guiding practitioners' intentions and actions. Wiccans believe that any magickal act must be aligned with the Rede, ensuring that it does not harm others or interfere with their free will. This principle has led to the development of ethical guidelines for spellwork, such as not performing love spells that infringe upon another's autonomy. The Rede reminds practitioners that their intentions and actions in the realm of magick carry ethical consequences and that personal responsibility is paramount.

Critics of the Rede argue that it oversimplifies the complex nature of ethical decision-making and the consequences of actions. They suggest that life is rarely so binary, and the Rede's emphasis on a strict threefold return can lead to a fear-based approach to spirituality. Some practitioners may become overly cautious or hesitant to take risks, fearing potential negative repercussions. Additionally, the Rede's deterministic nature implies a lack of free will, as individuals are bound to receive specific outcomes based solely on their actions.

Despite these criticisms, "Harm None" remains a foundational principle for many Wiccans and continues to influence their approach to magick, ritual, and daily life. It fosters an awareness of the interconnectedness of all living beings and encourages practitioners to strive for harmlessness and ethical behavior. It also serves as a cautionary reminder to approach the practice of magick with mindfulness and responsibility, as the energy one releases into the world can have far-reaching consequences.

In conclusion, "Harm None" is the ethical foundation of Wicca, encapsulated in the Wiccan Rede. It embodies harmlessness, personal responsibility, and respect for the interconnectedness of all life. The Rede serves as a moral compass that guides the actions, intentions, and choices of practitioners in ritual, spellwork, and daily life. While interpretations of the Rede may vary, its core principles of ethical consideration and reverence for the natural world continue to shape the moral compass of modern witches. Whether viewed as a cosmic justice system or a reminder of ethical considerations, "Harm None" underscores the importance of mindfulness and responsibility in the practice of Wicca, encouraging practitioners to navigate their spiritual journey with care and integrity.

Balancing Personal Will with Ethical Responsibility

Wicca, a modern pagan, witchcraft-based religion, places a strong emphasis on personal empowerment and the pursuit of one's will. At the same time, it carries a profound ethical principle encapsulated in the Wiccan Rede: "An it harm none, do what ye will." This juxtaposition between personal will and ethical responsibility lies at the core of Wiccan spirituality. It challenges practitioners to navigate the complex terrain of individual desires, intentions, and actions while upholding a commitment to harmlessness, personal responsibility, and respect for the interconnectedness of all life. To truly understand the delicate balance between personal will and ethical responsibility in Wicca, one must explore the intricacies of this ethical dilemma, its implications for Wiccan practice, and the ways in which Wiccans seek to harmonize their spiritual aspirations with their ethical convictions.

The Wiccan Rede, often pronounced as "reed," serves as a central ethical tenet within Wicca. While its origins are somewhat mysterious, it is closely associated with Gerald Gardner, a prominent figure in the early history of Wicca. Gardner introduced the Rede to a wider audience through his books, "Witchcraft Today" (1954) and "The Meaning of Witchcraft" (1959). However, the Rede's roots likely extend further back into the folkloric and witchcraft traditions of Britain, reflecting a broader ethos of harmlessness and personal responsibility.

The Rede's central message is succinct: "An it harm none, do what ye will." On the surface, it may seem to grant practitioners the freedom to pursue their desires and will without ethical restraint. However, a closer examination reveals a profound moral philosophy embedded within these words. The phrase "an it harm none" serves as a critical qualifier, placing a crucial condition on the pursuit of one's will. It emphasizes the importance of taking into account the potential harm or consequences of one's actions before proceeding.

This ethical guideline encourages practitioners to live their lives in harmony with the world around them, recognizing that their actions have an impact not only on themselves but also on others and the environment. It reflects the belief that every action has consequences and that ethical considerations should guide one's choices. The Rede calls for a deep awareness of the potential harm caused by one's actions and urges practitioners to choose paths that minimize or avoid harm altogether.

The delicate balance between personal will and ethical responsibility in Wicca is a subject of ongoing discussion and contemplation within the Wiccan community. One common interpretation of the Rede emphasizes the importance of personal responsibility. Practitioners are encouraged to weigh the potential consequences of their actions carefully and make choices that align with the highest ethical standards. This interpretation recognizes that life is complex, and ethical dilemmas can arise in various forms. It calls for a deep awareness of one's intentions and a commitment to minimizing harm whenever possible.

At the same time, this interpretation recognizes that personal will is a fundamental aspect of human existence. Wiccans believe that each individual has the right and the responsibility to pursue their own desires, dreams, and spiritual path. This empowerment is central to Wiccan spirituality, which places a strong emphasis on the individual's connection to the divine and the capacity to shape one's destiny.

This empowerment is particularly evident in Wiccan rituals and spellwork. Wiccans engage in magick, not to manipulate others or the natural world, but to align with their own desires, intentions, and goals. They view magick as a means of personal transformation, empowerment, and spiritual growth. The delicate balance between personal will and ethical responsibility is most apparent in the ethical guidelines that Wiccans adhere to when performing magick. For example, love spells that infringe upon another's free will or seek to manipulate their emotions are considered unethical, as they violate the principle of harmlessness and personal responsibility.

Another ethical consideration in Wiccan practice is the potential for unintended consequences. Practitioners recognize that the energy they release into the world through magickal workings can have far-reaching effects. This understanding highlights the importance of mindfulness and ethical consideration in all aspects of magick.

Critics of Wicca often argue that the Rede oversimplifies the complexities of ethical decision-making and the consequences of actions. They suggest that life rarely presents clear-cut choices between harm and harmlessness, and the Rede's emphasis on a strict threefold return can lead to a fear-based approach to spirituality. Some practitioners may become overly cautious or hesitant to take risks, fearing potential negative repercussions.

Despite these criticisms, "Balancing Personal Will with Ethical Responsibility" remains an essential aspect of Wiccan spirituality. It is a challenge that practitioners embrace as they seek to harmonize their desires, intentions, and actions with their ethical convictions. This balance underscores the interconnectedness of all life and the recognition that every choice has consequences that ripple through the web of existence.

In conclusion, the delicate balance between personal will and ethical responsibility is a central theme in Wicca, encapsulated in the Wiccan Rede: "An it harm none, do what ye will." This ethical principle challenges practitioners to navigate the complex terrain of individual desires, intentions, and actions while upholding a commitment to harmlessness, personal responsibility, and respect for the interconnectedness of all life. The interpretation of the Rede varies within the Wiccan community, but it ultimately underscores the importance of mindfulness and ethical consideration in all aspects of Wiccan practice. This balance allows practitioners to harness their personal empowerment while recognizing the ethical implications of their choices, fostering a deep sense of responsibility and connection to the world around them.

CHAPTER IV

The Wheel of the Year

Overview of the Eight Sabbats

In the Wiccan tradition, the Wheel of the Year serves as a sacred calendar, marking the passage of time and the changing seasons. This cycle is celebrated through eight major festivals known as Sabbats, each of which holds its unique significance, symbolism, and rituals. The Sabbats are a way for Wiccans to connect with nature's rhythms, honor the divine, and align their spiritual practice with the Earth's cycles. To gain a comprehensive understanding of the eight Sabbats, it is essential to explore their names, dates, associated themes, and the rituals that accompany these celebrations.

The first of the eight Sabbats is Samhain, which falls on October 31st or November 1st, depending on the tradition. Samhain marks the end of the old year and the beginning of the new one, making it a time of transition. It is often associated with death, ancestors, and the thinning of the veil between the physical and the spiritual realms. Wiccans may honor their deceased loved ones during Samhain and perform divination to seek guidance from the spirit world. Bonfires, feasting, and the carving of jack-o'-lanterns are common customs associated with this Sabbat.

Yule, also known as the Winter Solstice, occurs on or around December 21st. It is the longest night and the shortest day of the year, representing the rebirth of the Sun as the days gradually become longer. Yule is a time for celebrating the return of light and warmth to the world. Wiccans often exchange gifts, decorate evergreen trees, and light candles or a Yule log to symbolize the Sun's return. The theme of the rebirth of the God is central to Yule, as is the concept of hope and renewal.

Imbolc, occurring on February 1st or 2nd, marks the first stirrings of spring. It is associated with the Goddess Brigid and the concepts of purification, healing, and creativity. Imbolc is a time to prepare for the coming of spring and to bless and consecrate tools and objects used in Wiccan practice. It is also a celebration of the lengthening days and the promise of new life. Candlelight processions and the making of Brigid's crosses are common Imbolc traditions.

Ostara, also known as the Spring Equinox, falls around March 20th or 21st. It is a time of balance when day and night are of equal length. Ostara celebrates the awakening of the Earth and the fertility of the land. The Goddess and God are often honored during this Sabbat as symbols of growth and vitality. Eggs, symbols of fertility, are decorated, and the hare or rabbit, representing the Goddess, is associated with Ostara. Planting seeds, taking nature walks, and performing rituals to encourage personal growth are typical activities during this season. Beltane is celebrated on May 1st and indicates the beginning of summer. It is a Sabbat of passion, love, and fertility. Beltane celebrates the union of the God and Goddess, symbolizing the joining of the masculine and feminine energies in the natural world. Maypole dances, bonfires, and the weaving of flower crowns are common Beltane traditions. It is a time for revelry and joy, as well as for embracing one's desires and creativity.

Litha, also known as the Summer Solstice, occurs around June 20th or 21st and is the longest day and shortest night of the year. It celebrates the peak of the Sun's power and the abundance of nature. Litha is a time for honoring the God, who is at the height of his strength, and for embracing the fullness of life. Wiccans often gather in nature, light bonfires, and dance to celebrate the Sun's energy. Herbs, flowers, and other symbols of growth are central to Litha celebrations.

Lammas, also called Lughnasadh, takes place on August 1st or 2nd. It marks the first harvest of the year and is a time to give thanks for the abundance of the land. Lammas is associated with the Celtic God Lugh and the themes of sacrifice and rebirth. Wiccans may engage in the baking of bread and the sharing of food as a way to honor the Earth's bounty. It is also a time for personal reflection and setting intentions for the coming months. The last of the eight Sabbats is Mabon, the Autumn Equinox, which falls on or around September 21st or 22nd. It represents the balance between light and dark as the days become shorter and the nights longer. Mabon is a time to give thanks for the harvest, reflect on the past year, and prepare for the coming winter. Wiccans often create altars adorned with fruits, vegetables, and grains to symbolize the season's bounty. It is also a time for inner work, introspection, and finding balance in one's life.

Each Sabbat corresponds to a specific point in the natural cycle of the year, representing the changing seasons, the waxing and the waning of the Sun's power, and the growth and decline of the natural world. Wiccans celebrate these festivals to connect with these natural rhythms, honor the deities associated with each Sabbat, and perform rituals and spells that align with the themes of the season.

In addition to their specific themes and rituals, the Sabbats are often observed by casting a circle, a fundamental component of Wiccan ritual, and calling upon the energies of the four directions (North, East, South, West) and the elements (Earth, Air, Fire, Water) to create a sacred and protected space. The Wheel of the Year is seen as a continuous cycle, with each Sabbat flowing seamlessly into the next, reflecting the eternal cycles of life, death, and rebirth.

In conclusion, the eight Sabbats of Wicca are a testament to the religion's deep connection to nature, the changing seasons, and the spiritual significance of the natural world. Each Sabbat holds its unique symbolism and rituals, allowing Wiccans to honor the deities associated with the season and to connect with the cycles of the Earth. The Wheel of the Year provides a framework for Wiccans to celebrate the beauty and diversity of the natural world, fostering a deep sense of reverence, gratitude, and spiritual connection to the Earth and all its inhabitants.

Rituals and Celebrations for Each Sabbat

Wicca, a modern pagan, witchcraft-based religion, celebrates the Wheel of the Year through eight major festivals known as Sabbats. These Sabbats mark the passage of time, the changing seasons, and the spiritual significance of the natural world. Each Sabbat is a unique celebration, characterized by specific themes, rituals, and customs that allow Wiccans to connect with nature's rhythms, honor the deities associated with the season, and align their spiritual practice with the cycles of the Earth. In this section, we will delve into the rituals and celebrations associated with each of the eight Sabbats in Wicca.

The first of the eight Sabbats is Samhain, celebrated on October 31st or November 1st, depending on the tradition. Samhain marks the end of the old year and the beginning of the new one, making it a time of transition. It is often associated with death, ancestors, and the thinning of the veil between the physical and the spiritual realms. One of the central rituals of Samhain is the setting of an ancestor altar, where photographs, mementos, and offerings are placed to honor deceased loved ones. A feast, known as a Dumb Supper, is prepared and served in silence, allowing for communication with the spirits of the departed. Bonfires are lit to symbolize the light in the darkness, and divination practices, such as scrying and tarot readings, are commonly performed to seek guidance from the spirit world.

Yule, also known as the Winter Solstice, occurs on or around December 21st. It is the longest night and the shortest day of the year, symbolizing the rebirth of the Sun as the days gradually become longer. Yule is a time for celebrating the return of light and warmth to the world. One of the key rituals of Yule is the lighting of candles or a Yule log to symbolize the Sun's return. Many Wiccans exchange gifts, echoing the idea of giving and receiving light in the darkest time of the year. The God is often honored during this Sabbat, as his rebirth is a central theme. Feasting and singing songs that celebrate the return of the Sun are also common customs.

Imbolc, occurring on February 1st or 2nd, marks the first stirrings of spring. It is associated with the Goddess Brigid and themes of purification, healing, and creativity. One of the primary rituals of Imbolc is the lighting of candles to symbolize the increasing light and the Goddess's awakening from her winter slumber. It is also a time for blessings, and many Wiccans consecrate their tools and objects used in their spiritual practice during this Sabbat. Making Brigid's crosses, which are symbols of protection and blessings, is a traditional craft during this season. Imbolc emphasizes the return of life and the promise of new beginnings, making it a time for personal renewal and the planting of seeds, both metaphorical and literal.

Ostara, also known as the Spring Equinox, falls around March 20th or 21st. It is a time of balance when day and night are of equal length. Ostara celebrates the awakening of the Earth and the fertility of the land. One of the central rituals of Ostara is the creation of an Ostara egg, often elaborately decorated with symbols of fertility and growth. Planting seeds, taking nature walks, and performing rituals to encourage personal growth are typical activities during this season. The balance of light and dark is reflected in the honoring of the God and Goddess as equals during Ostara. As the Earth arouses from its winter slumber, Wiccans embrace the season of renewal and growth, focusing on new beginnings and the potential for transformation.

Beltane is celebrated on May 1st and indicates the beginning of summer. It is a Sabbat of passion, love, and fertility. Beltane celebrates the union of the God and Goddess, symbolizing the joining of the masculine and feminine energies in the natural world. A central Beltane ritual is the Maypole dance, where participants weave colorful ribbons around a tall pole, symbolizing the intertwining of life and love. Bonfires are lit to honor the Sun's growing power and to symbolize the passion and desire of the season. The making of flower crowns and the decoration of May baskets filled with flowers are also common customs. Beltane is a time for revelry, joy, and embracing one's desires and creativity.

Litha, also known as the Summer Solstice, occurs around June 20th or 21st and is the longest day and shortest night of the year. It celebrates the peak of the Sun's power and the abundance of nature. One of the central rituals of Litha is the lighting of bonfires and candles to honor the Sun's energy and to acknowledge the fullness of life. Herbs, flowers, and other symbols of growth are often incorporated into rituals and decorations. Litha is a time for joyous celebration, with gatherings in nature, dancing, and feasting. It is also a time for personal reflection and setting intentions for the coming months.

Lammas, also called Lughnasadh, takes place on August 1st or 2nd. It marks the first harvest of the year and is a time to give thanks for the abundance of the land. Lammas is associated with the Celtic God Lugh and the themes of sacrifice and rebirth. One of the central rituals of Lammas is the baking of bread from the first harvested grains, symbolizing the God's sacrifice for the land and the cycle of life, death, and rebirth. Many Wiccans also engage in the sharing of food, emphasizing the importance of community and gratitude. Lammas is a time for personal reflection on the sacrifices made in one's life and the promise of new opportunities that arise from them.

The last of the eight Sabbats is Mabon, the Autumn Equinox, which falls on or around September 21st or 22nd. It represents the balance between light and dark as the days become shorter and the nights longer. Mabon is a time to give thanks for the harvest, reflect on the past year, and prepare for the coming winter. One of the central rituals of Mabon is the creation of an altar adorned with fruits, vegetables, and grains to symbolize the season's bounty. Wiccans often engage in rituals that focus on gratitude and introspection, recognizing the importance of finding balance in one's life. It is a time to gather with loved ones, share the fruits of the harvest, and express gratitude for the Earth's abundance.

In conclusion, the eight Sabbats in Wicca offer a rich tapestry of rituals and celebrations that reflect the changing seasons, the cycles of life, and the spiritual significance of the natural world. Each Sabbat has its unique themes and customs, allowing Wiccans to honor the deities associated with the season and to connect with the rhythms of the Earth. These celebrations foster a deep sense of reverence, gratitude, and spiritual connection to the Earth and all its inhabitants, encouraging personal growth, reflection, and the harmonious integration of the spiritual and natural worlds.

The Spiritual Significance of the Wheel of the Year

The Wheel of the Year is a sacred and intricate concept at the heart of Wicca, a modern pagan, witchcraft-based religion. It represents the cyclical nature of time, the changing seasons, and the interconnectedness of all life. Through the celebration of eight major festivals known as Sabbats, Wiccans honor the spiritual significance of the Wheel of the Year, aligning their practice with the rhythms of the Earth and the divine forces of nature. These celebrations offer a profound opportunity for personal growth, spiritual connection, and a deepening understanding of the interconnected web of existence.

At its core, the Wheel of the Year embodies the idea that life is a continuous cycle of birth, growth, death, and rebirth. This cycle mirrors the natural world's patterns, from the blossoming of spring to the harvest of autumn and the restful slumber of winter. Each phase of the Wheel carries its unique energy, symbolism, and lessons, allowing Wiccans to explore the depths of their spirituality and interact with the divine in various ways.

The eight Sabbats that make up the Wheel of the Year are Samhain, Yule, Imbolc, Ostara, Beltane, Litha, Lammas, and Mabon. These festivals are spaced evenly throughout the year and mark key points in the natural cycle. By observing the Sabbats, Wiccans honor the changing seasons and the unique qualities associated with each phase of the Wheel. This connection to nature fosters a sense of reverence and respect for the Earth and its rhythms.

Samhain, celebrated on October 31st or November 1st, marks the beginning of the Wheel and represents death and rebirth. It is a time when the veil between the physical and the spiritual worlds is thin, allowing for communication with ancestors and spirits. Samhain teaches us to embrace change and acknowledge the interconnectedness of life and death. It reminds us that death is not the end but a part of the eternal cycle of existence.

Yule, the Winter Solstice, occurring around December 21st, symbolizes the return of light and hope in the darkest time of the year. Yule teaches us that even in the depths of winter, there is the promise of renewal and the return of the Sun. It encourages us to find light in our lives, even in the darkest of times, and to celebrate the power of rebirth.

Imbolc, celebrated on February 1st or 2nd, represents the first stirrings of spring and the arousing of the Earth. It teaches us the importance of purification and renewal as we get ready for the coming of new life. Imbolc encourages us to let go of the past and make room for growth and transformation.

Ostara, the Spring Equinox, occurs around March 20th or 21st and symbolizes balance and fertility. It teaches us to embrace the harmony between light and dark, day and night, and the masculine and feminine energies. Ostara encourages us to celebrate the Earth's awakening and the potential for new beginnings.

Beltane, celebrated on May 1st, embodies passion, love, and union. It teaches us to honor our desires and embrace the joy of life. Beltane encourages us to celebrate love in all its forms and to recognize the power of connection and unity.

Litha, the Summer Solstice, occurs around June 20th or 21st and symbolizes the peak of the Sun's power and the abundance of nature. It teaches us to revel in the fullness of life and to appreciate the beauty of the natural world. Litha encourages us to celebrate our vitality and to acknowledge the interconnectedness of all living things.

Lammas, celebrated on August 1st or 2nd, represents the first harvest of the year and the concept of sacrifice and rebirth. It teaches us to give thanks for the Earth's bounty and to recognize the cycles of life, death, and renewal. Lammas encourages us to let go of what no longer serves us and to make way for new opportunities.

Mabon, the Autumn Equinox, occurs around September 21st or 22nd and symbolizes balance and reflection. It teaches us to find equilibrium in our lives and to give thanks for the harvest, both literal and metaphorical. Mabon encourages us to reflect on our journey and to prepare for the season of rest and introspection.

The spiritual significance of the Wheel of the Year extends beyond the individual Sabbats. It underscores the idea that life is a continuous journey of growth, change, and transformation. Each phase of the Wheel invites us to reflect on our own spiritual path and to connect with the energies of the natural world. By aligning our practice with the Wheel, we deepen our relationship with the divine and gain a greater understanding of our place in the interconnected web of existence.

The Wheel also emphasizes the importance of balance and harmony. As we move through the seasons, we witness the dance of opposites—light and dark, life and death, growth and decline. This balance is reflected in the Sabbats themselves, where dualities are celebrated and embraced. By recognizing the interplay of opposites, we learn to find equilibrium in our own lives and honor the diversity and interconnectedness of all life.

Moreover, the Wheel of the Year provides a framework for personal and spiritual growth. Each phase offers its unique lessons and challenges, inviting us to explore different aspects of ourselves and our spirituality. For example, Samhain teaches us about letting go and embracing change, while Beltane encourages us to celebrate love and passion. By engaging with these lessons, we evolve and deepen our connection to the divine.

In conclusion, the Wheel of the Year is a profound and spiritually significant concept in Wicca. It represents the cyclical nature of time, the changing seasons, and the interconnectedness of all life. Through the celebration of the eight Sabbats, Wiccans honor the natural cycle and align their practice with the divine forces of nature. The Wheel teaches us the importance of balance, reflection, and personal growth, fostering a deep sense of reverence, connection, and harmony with the Earth and all its inhabitants. It reminds us that we are part of a greater whole, bound by the eternal cycles of life, death, and rebirth.

CHAPTER V

The Wiccan Ritual Structure

Casting the Circle

Casting the circle is a fundamental and sacred practice in Wicca, a modern pagan, witchcraft-based religion. It is a ritual act that serves to create a sacred and protected space in which Wiccans can perform their rituals, commune with the divine, and work magick. The circle is seen as a boundary between the mundane world and the spiritual realm, a place where the energies of the ritual are focused and contained. To understand the significance of casting the circle in Wicca, it is essential to explore the mechanics of the ritual, its purpose, and the symbolism behind it.

The act of casting the circle typically begins with the practitioner facing the north, where the circle will be anchored. In many Wiccan traditions, a ceremonial tool, such as a wand or an athame (ritual knife), is used to physically trace the circumference of the circle. The practitioner moves clockwise (deosil) around the designated space, visualizing a protective barrier forming as they do so. While casting the circle, it is common to recite specific words or invocations that call upon the elements, the quarters (north, east, south, west), and the deities to aid in the circle's creation and protection.

The circle itself can be visualized as a sphere of energy extending both above and below the physical plane. It acts as a barrier that separates the sacred space within from the outside world. The circle is not a physical barrier but a metaphysical one, symbolizing the interconnectedness of all things while providing a contained space for magickal and spiritual work. This practice ensures that the energies raised and the entities summoned during the ritual remain within the circle, preventing any interference from external influences.

The circle's purpose in Wicca is multifaceted and holds deep spiritual significance. One primary purpose is to create a space in which the practitioner can connect with the divine, whether that be the God and Goddess, elemental spirits, ancestors, or other entities. By casting the circle, Wiccans create a bridge between the physical and the spiritual realms, allowing for communion with higher powers and the flow of divine energy.

Another vital function of the circle is to concentrate and amplify the energy generated during rituals. It acts as a container that holds the energy until it is ready to be released towards a specific goal or intention. This concentrated energy is often used in spellwork, divination, healing, or other magickal workings. The circle's boundaries prevent energy from dissipating into the surrounding environment, ensuring that it remains focused and potent.

Symbolically, the circle represents the cycle of life, death, and rebirth—the fundamental concept at the heart of Wicca. It is a reflection of the eternal nature of the soul, which continues to evolve and grow through successive lifetimes. The casting of the circle mirrors the cyclical nature of the seasons, the phases of the Moon, and the cycles of birth and death. It serves as a reminder of the interconnectedness of all life and the eternal movement of creation and transformation.

Each quarter of the circle, associated with the elements of Earth, Air, Fire, and Water, holds specific symbolism and energies. The practitioner often calls upon these elements when casting the circle to invoke their qualities and attributes. The North, associated with Earth, represents stability, grounding, and physical manifestation. The East, associated with Air, embodies intellect, communication, and inspiration. The South, associated with Fire, symbolizes passion, transformation, and willpower. The West, associated with Water, represents emotions, intuition, and healing. By invoking these elements, Wiccans seek to create a harmonious and balanced sacred space.

Casting the circle also serves as a form of purification and consecration. Before entering the circle, many practitioners perform a cleansing ritual to purify themselves of negative energies and distractions. Once inside the circle, the energies are considered to be in a state of heightened purity and readiness for magickal or spiritual work. The act of casting the circle reinforces the idea that the space within is sanctified and dedicated to the sacred purpose at hand.

In addition to the act of casting the circle, Wiccans often call upon the deities, ancestors, or elemental spirits to guard and watch over the circle. This is typically done by invoking the energies or entities associated with each quarter. For example, the God and Goddess may be invoked at the center of the circle to preside over the ritual. The practitioner may also invite specific deities or spirits related to the ritual's purpose. These guardians are seen as protectors and guides, ensuring that the circle remains a safe and sacred space.

Once the circle has been cast and the ritual work is complete, it is customary to "open" or "release" the circle. This is done by moving counterclockwise (widdershins) around the circle, often with a specific closing ritual or words of thanks. The act of opening the circle symbolizes the release of energies, the dissolution of the protective barrier, and the return to the mundane world. It is a way of bringing closure to the ritual and acknowledging that the sacred space has served its purpose.

While casting the circle is a central practice in Wicca, it is not limited to this tradition alone. Similar practices can be found in various forms of modern witchcraft and pagan spirituality. The concept of creating sacred space and working within a protected and consecrated environment is a universal principle in many spiritual and magickal traditions.

In conclusion, casting the circle is a foundational and spiritually significant practice in Wicca. It serves to create a sacred and protected space where Wiccans can communicate with the divine, work magick, and commune with higher powers. The circle symbolizes the cycle of life, death, and rebirth, and acts as a container for concentrated energy. It embodies the interconnectedness of all life and the eternal dance of creation and transformation. Casting the circle is a ritual of purification, consecration, and protection, ensuring that the energies raised remain focused and potent. It is a practice that fosters reverence, connection, and a deepening of one's spiritual path within the framework of Wicca.

Invoking Deity

In the practice of Wicca, the connection with the divine is at the core of spiritual experience. Wiccans believe in a pantheon of deities, which can vary from one tradition or individual to another, reflecting a diverse range of spiritual perspectives. These deities, often associated with archetypal energies and natural forces, are honored and invoked in rituals to seek guidance, empowerment, and a deepening of the practitioner's spiritual connection. The act of invoking deity is a sacred and profound practice that allows Wiccans to tap into the divine energies, whether it be the God and Goddess of the tradition or specific deities associated with the intended purpose of the ritual. In this section, we will delve into the significance, methods, and spiritual implications of invoking deity in Wicca.

At the heart of Wiccan spirituality lies the belief in a duality of the divine, typically represented by the God and Goddess. These deities embody complementary aspects of existence, such as the masculine and feminine, the light and dark, and the creative and destructive forces of nature. The God represents the masculine aspect and is often associated with the Sun, the hunt, and the cycle of life, death, and rebirth. The Goddess represents the feminine aspect and is often associated with the Moon, fertility, and the nurturing and transformative energies of the Earth. These deities are seen as partners in a divine dance, reflecting the interconnectedness and balance found in the natural world.

The act of invoking deity is a means of establishing a direct connection with these divine energies. It is a way for Wiccans to commune with the God and Goddess, seeking their guidance, blessings, and assistance in magickal workings or spiritual endeavors. Invocation is not seen as an attempt to control or manipulate the deities but as an act of reverence and communion. It is an invitation for the divine to be present in the ritual, to share in the energies of the sacred space, and to offer their wisdom and support.

The process of invoking deity in Wicca is a structured and ritualized practice. It typically begins with the casting of the circle, a sacred space where the energies are focused and contained. Once the circle is cast and purified, the practitioner or a designated priest or priestess may recite invocations specific to the deities being called upon. These invocations are often poetic and evocative, describing the attributes and qualities of the God and Goddess and inviting their presence into the circle.

The invocations may take various forms, such as prayers, chants, or spoken words, depending on the tradition and personal preference. They often acknowledge the deity's role in the cycle of the seasons, the mysteries of life and death, and their relevance to the specific purpose of the ritual. For example, in a fertility ritual, the invocation may emphasize the Goddess's role as a fertile and nurturing mother, while in a Samhain (or Halloween) ritual, the focus may shift to the God's role as the guide of souls into the afterlife.

In some Wiccan traditions, invocations are accompanied by physical actions or gestures, such as drawing down the Moon or the Sun. Drawing down the Moon is a ritual in which the priestess invokes the Goddess's presence into herself, allowing her to speak and act as the Goddess during the ritual. Similarly, drawing down the Sun is a ritual in which the priest invokes the God's presence, embodying his energies and wisdom. These rituals are powerful acts of divine communion, providing a direct channel for the energies of the deities to flow through the practitioner.

As the deities are invoked, their energies are believed to infuse the sacred space, transforming it into a place of heightened spiritual significance. This infusion of divine energy is tangible to many Wiccans, often accompanied by a sense of presence, warmth, or emotional resonance. The practitioner may experience a deepening of their own connection to the deities, feeling the divine energies as a source of empowerment and guidance.

The presence of the deities is not limited to the duration of the ritual; they are often seen as companions and guides in daily life. Wiccans may develop personal relationships with the God and Goddess, communicating with them through meditation, prayer, or divination. These interactions are considered sacred and deeply personal, providing insight, support, and a sense of divine presence in the practitioner's life.

In addition to invoking the God and Goddess, Wiccans may also work with specific deities from various pantheons, depending on the tradition or the intent of the ritual. These deities may be chosen for their relevance to a particular aspect of the practitioner's life or magickal working. For example, a practitioner seeking love and passion may invoke Aphrodite or Eros, while someone seeking wisdom and guidance may invoke Athena or Hermes. These deity-specific rituals often involve extensive research, study, and understanding of the chosen deity's mythology and attributes.

The act of invoking deity carries deep spiritual implications in Wicca. It emphasizes the belief in the divine as immanent, meaning that the divine is present and accessible within the natural world and the practitioner's own being. It challenges the idea of a distant and transcendent deity and instead invites a direct and personal relationship with the divine energies of the God and Goddess. This approach fosters a sense of empowerment, autonomy, and responsibility for one's own spiritual growth and development.

Moreover, invoking deity serves as a reminder of the interconnectedness of all life and the recognition that divinity exists in the world around us. The deities of Wicca are often associated with natural forces, such as the cycles of the Moon, the changing seasons, and the elements. By working with these deities, Wiccans align themselves with the natural world, acknowledging their role as stewards of the Earth and the sacredness of all living things.

In conclusion, invoking deity is a profound and sacred practice in Wicca that allows practitioners to connect with the divine energies of the God and Goddess or specific deities. It is a structured and ritualized act of communion, inviting the presence and guidance of the divine into the sacred space of the circle. This practice carries deep spiritual significance, emphasizing the immanence of the divine, the interconnectedness of all life, and the empowerment of the individual practitioner. It fosters a direct and personal relationship with the divine, providing insight, support, and a sense of divine presence in both ritual and daily life. Invocation is a powerful means of deepening one's spiritual connection, seeking guidance, and aligning with the natural forces and energies that shape the world.

Spellwork and Magick in Wiccan Rituals

In the realm of Wiccan spirituality, spellwork and magick serve as powerful tools for manifesting intentions, seeking spiritual growth, and connecting with the divine. Central to Wiccan practice, spellwork involves the intentional manipulation of energy to create change, while magick encompasses a broader concept of harnessing natural forces and energies to influence the world around us. These practices are deeply intertwined with Wiccan rituals, offering a means to transform desires, heal, protect, and commune with the divine. In this section, we will delve into the significance, methods, and ethical considerations surrounding spellwork and magick in Wicca.

Spellwork in Wicca is the art of manifesting desires or intentions through the focused use of energy and intent. It is a way for practitioners to actively engage with the natural forces and energies that surround them, aligning their will with their desired outcomes. Spells can take various forms, including candle magick, herbal magick, crystal magick, and many others, each utilizing specific tools and correspondences to enhance the effectiveness of the spell.

One of the central components of spellwork is intention setting. Wiccans believe that intent is a crucial element in magick, as it directs the energy and purpose of the spell.

Before casting a spell, practitioners often take time to clearly define their intentions, specifying what they want to achieve and why. This process of intention setting helps focus the practitioner's will and energy, aligning them with the desired outcome.

Candle magick is one of the most common forms of spellwork in Wicca. It involves the use of colored candles, each corresponding to different intentions or purposes. The practitioner may anoint the candle with oils, carve symbols or words into the wax, and charge it with their intent. The candle is then lit during a ritual, and as it burns, it releases the energy and intention into the universe. The choice of candle color, the symbolism of the carved designs, and the specific words spoken during the ritual all contribute to the spell's efficacy.

Herbal magick involves the use of herbs and plants with specific correspondences to enhance spellwork. Practitioners may create sachets, incense blends, or infusions using herbs that align with their intentions. For instance, rosemary is often used for protection, while lavender is associated with relaxation and peace. The practitioner may also use herbal correspondences in the form of smudging or sprinkling herbs to purify and consecrate a sacred space before spellcasting.

Crystal magick utilizes the energetic properties of crystals and gemstones to enhance spells and rituals. Each crystal is associated with different energies and intentions. For instance, amethyst is often used for spiritual growth and clarity, while rose quartz is associated with love and healing. Practitioners may carry crystals with them, place them on altars, or incorporate them into talismans or jewelry to amplify their intentions.

Another common form of spellwork is sigil magick. In this practice, practitioners create a unique symbol, or sigil, that represents their intention. The sigil is charged with energy, often through meditation or visualization, and then released into the universe. The act of creating and charging a sigil is a deeply personal and symbolic process, reinforcing the practitioner's connection to their intention.

Magick, as a broader concept in Wicca, encompasses not only spellwork but also the utilization of ritual and symbolism to communicate with the divine and harness natural energies. Rituals in Wicca are structured ceremonies that may include various components such as invocations, offerings, and symbolic acts. These rituals are designed to make a sacred and focused space where practitioners can work with the energies of the universe and the divine.

A central aspect of Wiccan rituals is the calling of the quarters. In this practice, the practitioner or the coven acknowledges and invokes the energies associated with the four cardinal directions: north (earth), east (air), south (fire), and west (water). Each direction holds specific correspondences and qualities that contribute to the ritual's intention. By calling upon these energies, practitioners seek to create a balanced and harmonious sacred space.

Rituals in Wicca often involve the use of tools such as athames (ritual knives), wands, chalices, and pentacles. These tools are consecrated and charged with energy, serving as conduits for directing and focusing magickal energy during the ritual. For example, an athame may be used to cast a circle or to symbolically direct energy, while a chalice may hold a libation for the deities.

The use of symbolism is also prevalent in Wiccan magick. Practitioners often incorporate correspondences, such as colors, herbs, and crystals, into their rituals to amplify the energies and intentions of the spell. Symbols and sacred geometry, such as the pentacle or the triple moon symbol, are used to represent spiritual concepts and connect with the divine.

Wiccans may also work with the phases of the Moon in their magickal practices. The lunar cycle is seen as a reflection of the natural rhythms and cycles of life. Different phases of the Moon are linked with specific intentions and energies. For instance, the waxing Moon is a time for growth and manifestation, while the waning Moon is suitable for banishing and releasing. Many Wiccans time their spells and rituals to coincide with the appropriate lunar phase to enhance their effectiveness.

The ethical considerations surrounding spellwork and magick in Wicca are integral to the practice. Wiccans adhere to the ethical principle known as the "Threefold Law" or the "Law of Return," which states that the energy one puts into the universe will return to them threefold. This principle emphasizes the responsibility of practitioners to use magick for positive and constructive purposes, avoiding harm to others or oneself.

Ethical considerations also extend to issues of consent and free will. Practitioners are discouraged from using magick to manipulate or control others against their will. Respect for individual autonomy and the recognition of the consequences of one's actions are paramount in Wiccan ethics.

Additionally, practitioners are encouraged to perform divination or meditation before engaging in spellwork to gain clarity and insight into their intentions. This process helps ensure that the intentions are in alignment with one's higher self and are not driven by ego, fear, or negative emotions.

In conclusion, spellwork and magick in Wiccan rituals are powerful means of manifesting intentions, seeking spiritual growth, and connecting with the divine. These practices involve the intentional manipulation of energy and the use of tools, correspondences, and symbolism to amplify the practitioner's intent. Rituals in Wicca create a sacred and focused space in which practitioners can work with natural forces and energies. Ethical considerations, such as the Threefold Law and respect for free will, are integral to Wiccan magick, emphasizing the importance of using magick for positive and constructive purposes. Spellwork and magick in Wicca are not only practical tools but also profound spiritual practices that foster a more profound connection with the natural world and the divine.

Cakes and Ale: Sharing in the Divine

In the rich tapestry of Wiccan rituals, the practice of "Cakes and Ale" holds a special place. This simple yet profound ritual act is a means for Wiccans to share in the divine, acknowledge the sacredness of sustenance, and foster a sense of community. Cakes and Ale, also known as "Cakes and Wine," are an integral part of many Wiccan rituals, particularly those that celebrate the Wheel of the Year and other significant occasions. This practice not only nourishes the body but also feeds the spirit, connecting participants with the energies of the Earth and the deities. In this section, we will delve into the significance, symbolism, and ritual aspects of Cakes and Ale in Wicca.

The practice of Cakes and Ale centers around the sharing of food and drink within the sacred circle. It is a communal act that symbolizes the interconnectedness of all life and the divine energies that sustain it. While the specific foods and beverages used may vary among traditions and individuals, the underlying symbolism remains consistent. Cakes are typically small, baked goods, such as cookies or bread, while ale can be any form of liquid refreshment, such as wine, mead, or juice. These offerings are often chosen for their symbolism and correspondences, aligning with the intention and purpose of the ritual.

One of the central elements of Cakes and Ale is the act of consecration. Before the ritual begins, the cakes and ale are blessed and consecrated, often through the use of words, gestures, or invocations. This act charges the offerings with the divine energy and intention of the ritual, transforming them from ordinary sustenance into sacred nourishment. The consecration may involve calling upon the deities, the elements, or the energies of the Earth to infuse the food and drink with their blessings and power.

The sharing of Cakes and Ale typically occurs at a specific point in the ritual, often toward the end, after the main magickal workings or invocations have taken place. The participants within the sacred circle take a piece of cake and a sip of ale, symbolizing the sharing of the divine energy and the unity of the group. This act fosters a sense of communion and connection among the participants, reinforcing the idea that they are all part of a larger whole.

The symbolism of Cakes and Ale in Wicca is multifaceted and deeply rooted in spiritual concepts. The cakes represent the Earth and the physical realm, while the ale symbolizes the waters of life and the spiritual realm. The act of partaking in these offerings acknowledges the sacredness of the Earth and the divine energies that flow through it. It reinforces the belief that all life is interconnected, and that the physical and spiritual realms are intimately linked.

The sharing of Cakes and Ale is also a way to honor the deities and the energies of the ritual. In Wicca, the deities are often associated with the cycles of life, death, and rebirth. By consuming the offerings, participants symbolically become one with the deities, acknowledging their presence and inviting their blessings into their lives. This act of communion reinforces the belief that the divine is immanent, present in all aspects of existence.

Moreover, Cakes and Ale serve as a form of grounding and centering after the heightened energy of a ritual. The act of eating and drinking helps to bring participants back to a state of balance and physical awareness. It allows them to integrate the energies raised during the ritual into their physical bodies, fostering a sense of peace and connection with the Earth.

The symbolism of Cakes and Ale is further enriched by the concept of the "Great Rite." In some Wiccan traditions, the act of sharing Cakes and Ale is seen as a symbolic reenactment of the Great Rite, a sacred union between the God and Goddess. The athame (ritual knife) is often used to bless and cut the cake, symbolizing the union of the God and Goddess, while the chalice represents the womb of the Goddess. This symbolism reinforces the idea that all of life is a reflection of the divine union and the cyclical nature of existence.

Ethical considerations also play a role in the practice of Cakes and Ale. Wiccans adhere to the ethical principle known as the "Threefold Law" or the "Law of Return," which states that the energy one puts into the universe will return to them threefold. This principle emphasizes the responsibility of practitioners to use magick and ritual for positive and constructive purposes. When sharing Cakes and Ale, participants are encouraged to focus on intentions that align with the principles of love, healing, and empowerment, avoiding harm to others or oneself.

In addition to its spiritual significance, the practice of Cakes and Ale fosters a sense of community and belonging among participants. Sharing in a sacred meal creates a bond among those within the sacred circle, reinforcing the idea that they are all part of a larger spiritual family. This sense of community is an essential aspect of many Wiccan covens and gatherings, providing support, friendship, and a sense of shared purpose.

Cakes and Ale also serve as a form of offering and gratitude to the deities and the Earth. By sharing the fruits of the Earth and the blessings of the divine, participants express their thanks and reverence for the abundance of the natural world. This act of giving and receiving reinforces the idea that the Earth is a source of sustenance and nourishment, and that gratitude is a fundamental aspect of Wiccan spirituality.

In conclusion, the practice of Cakes and Ale in Wicca is a sacred and communal act that symbolizes the sharing of the divine, the interconnectedness of all life, and the unity of the physical and spiritual realms. It is a means of grounding and centering after ritual work, a form of offering and gratitude to the deities and the Earth, and a way to foster a sense of community and connection among participants. This practice holds deep symbolism and spiritual significance, reinforcing the belief that all of life is sacred and that the divine is immanent in the world around us. Cakes and Ale are more than just food and drink; they are a means of nourishing the body and soul, a reminder of our connection to the Earth, and a celebration of the divine within and around us.

CHAPTER VI

The Elements and Their Correspondences

Earth, Air, Fire, Water, and Spirit

In the intricate tapestry of Wiccan spirituality, the elemental forces of Earth, Air, Fire, Water, and Spirit occupy a central and revered place. These elements are not merely physical substances but symbolic representations of profound spiritual concepts, energies, and archetypal forces that are woven into the very fabric of the natural world. Wiccans believe that these elements are not only present in the external world but also within themselves, and that by working with and understanding these elemental forces, they can deepen their spiritual connection, bring balance to their lives, and manifest their intentions. In this section, we will delve into the significance, symbolism, and spiritual aspects of Earth, Air, Fire, Water, and Spirit in Wicca.

The element of Earth is linked with stability, grounding, and the physical realm. It represents the solid and tangible aspects of existence—the land beneath our feet, the rocks, crystals, and plants that grow from it. In Wiccan rituals, Earth is often represented by salt or soil, and its color is typically green or brown. Earth's energies are considered nurturing and supportive, providing a sense of security and stability.

Working with the element of Earth involves connecting with the physical body and the material world. It is a reminder of our connection to the Earth and the importance of tending to our physical needs. Wiccans often call upon Earth's energies for grounding and stability, especially when they need to center themselves or when their energies are scattered. This connection to Earth is also vital in magick, as it helps manifest intentions into the physical realm.

The element of Air is linked with intellect, communication, and the realm of thought and ideas. It represents the intangible but essential aspects of existence—the air we breathe, the winds that carry our thoughts and words. In Wiccan rituals, Air is often represented by incense smoke or feathers, and its color is typically yellow or white. Air's energies are considered to be cleansing and invigorating, aiding in mental clarity and communication.

Working with the element of Air involves tapping into the realm of thoughts and ideas. It is a reminder of the power of words, both spoken and unspoken, and the importance of clear communication. Wiccans often call upon Air's energies when they seek inspiration, guidance, or clarity of thought. This connection to Air is also crucial in spellwork, as it helps imbue intentions with mental focus and direction.

The element of Fire is linked with transformation, passion, and the realm of action and willpower. It represents the fiery and dynamic aspects of existence—the flames that ignite change and drive action. In Wiccan rituals, Fire is often represented by a candle or a lit brazier, and its color is typically red or orange. Fire's energies are considered purifying and energizing, fueling creativity and passion.

Working with the element of Fire involves harnessing the energy of transformation and change. It is a reminder of the power of action and the importance of maintaining one's inner flame. Wiccans often call upon Fire's energies when they need motivation, courage, or when they seek to bring about change in their lives. This connection to

Fire is also integral in spellwork, as it helps manifest intentions through the power of will.

The element of Water is linked with emotions, intuition, and the realm of feelings and dreams. It represents the fluid and adaptable aspects of existence—the waters that flow within and around us. In Wiccan rituals, Water is often represented by a chalice filled with water or a cauldron, and its color is typically blue or silver. Water's energies are considered calming and purifying, aiding in emotional healing and intuition.

Working with the element of Water involves connecting with the depths of one's emotions and intuition. It is a reminder of the importance of understanding and honoring one's feelings and inner guidance. Wiccans often call upon Water's energies when they seek emotional healing, insight, or when they wish to enhance their psychic abilities. This connection to Water is also significant in spellwork, as it helps imbue intentions with emotional depth and intuition.

The element of Spirit, also known as Akasha or Ether, is often considered the fifth element in Wicca, though it transcends the physical elements. It represents unity, divine connection, and the realm of the soul and spiritual essence. Spirit is the unifying force that connects all things and infuses them with life. It is often associated with the color white, black, or purple. Spirit's energies are considered transcendent and all-encompassing, aligning with the divine source.

Working with the element of Spirit involves connecting with the divine essence within oneself and recognizing the interconnectedness of all life. It is a reminder of the sacredness of existence and the importance of seeking spiritual growth and understanding. Wiccans often call upon Spirit's energies for guidance, inspiration, and to connect with higher consciousness. Spirit is also invoked to bless and consecrate rituals, tools, and sacred spaces, as it represents the divine presence that resides within all things.

In Wiccan rituals and magickal workings, practitioners often call upon the energies of these elements to create a balanced and harmonious sacred space. This is often done by acknowledging and invoking the energies of the four cardinal directions, each associated with one of the elements. For example, the North is associated with Earth, the East with Air, the South with Fire, and the West with Water. By calling upon these elemental energies, Wiccans seek to create a balanced and harmonious sacred space where they can connect with the divine, work magick, and seek guidance.

Moreover, the concept of the "Pentacle" or "Pentagram" is a powerful symbol in Wicca that represents the interconnectedness of these five elements. The pentacle is a five-pointed star within a circle, with each point representing one of the elements—Earth, Air, Fire, Water, and Spirit. The circle represents the unity and the interconnectedness of these elements, and the pentacle is often used as a magickal tool for protection, balance, and manifestation.

In conclusion, the elements of Earth, Air, Fire, Water, and Spirit hold profound spiritual significance in Wicca, representing various aspects of existence and the interconnectedness of all life. These elements are not just symbolic but are believed to be present within the practitioner, the natural world, and the divine. Working with these elemental forces allows Wiccans to deepen their spiritual connection, bring balance to their lives, and manifest their intentions. The elements are invoked and honored in Wiccan rituals and magickal workings, creating a sacred and harmonious space in which practitioners can commune with the divine and seek spiritual growth. They are a reminder of the sacredness of existence and the interconnectedness of all life, guiding Wiccans on their spiritual journey and fostering a deeper understanding of the natural world and the divine within and around us.

How the Elements Influence Wiccan Practice

In the intricate tapestry of Wiccan spirituality, the elements of Earth, Air, Fire, Water, and Spirit play a profound and guiding role. These elemental forces are not merely abstract concepts but are seen as tangible and sacred aspects of the natural world, each holding unique qualities and energies that influence Wiccan practice. The relationship between Wiccans and the elements is one of deep reverence, as they believe that these forces are not only present in the external world but also within themselves. In this section, we will delve into how the elements influence Wiccan practice, shaping rituals, magickal workings, and the spiritual journey of practitioners.

The elements are integral to the creation of sacred space in Wiccan practice. When casting a circle—a fundamental ritual act that defines a sacred and protected area— Wiccans often call upon the energies associated with the four cardinal directions, each linked to one of the elements. The North corresponds to Earth, the East to Air, the South to Fire, and the West to Water. By invoking these elemental energies, practitioners create a balanced and harmonious space where they can connect with the divine, perform magickal workings, and seek guidance. The elemental associations of the directions provide a framework for the structure of the circle. The North, associated with Earth, represents stability and grounding, anchoring the energies of the circle. The East, associated with Air, represents intellect and communication, fostering mental clarity and focused intent. The South, linked to Fire, embodies transformation and passion, infusing the circle with energy and motivation. The West, connected to Water, represents emotions and intuition, providing a sense of emotional balance and inner guidance.

In Wiccan magick, the elements play a significant role in shaping the intention and outcome of spells and rituals. Practitioners often choose specific elements to correspond with their magickal goals. For example, if one is seeking to manifest stability and abundance in their life, they may work with the element of Earth. To enhance mental clarity and communication, the element of Air may be invoked. When aiming to fuel creativity and passion, Fire is a fitting choice, and for emotional healing and intuition, Water is a suitable ally.

The elements are also integrated into the tools and correspondences used in magickal workings. Ritual tools such as athames (ritual knives), wands, chalices, and pentacles are often associated with specific elements. For instance, the athame may represent Fire or the will, while the chalice symbolizes Water or emotions. These tools are consecrated and charged with elemental energies, serving as conduits for directing and focusing magickal energy during rituals.

One of the most potent symbols in Wicca is the pentacle or pentagram—a five-pointed star within a circle. Each point of the star represents one of the elements—Earth, Air, Fire, Water, and Spirit—and the circle symbolizes the unity and interconnectedness of these forces. The pentacle is often used as a magickal tool for protection, balance, and manifestation.

Wiccans may use the pentacle in various ways during rituals and magickal workings. Placing it on an altar or within the sacred circle aligns the practitioner with the elemental energies and serves as a reminder of their sacred connection to the natural world and the divine. Drawing the pentacle in the air with a wand or athame can be a gesture of invoking or banishing specific elemental energies as needed in the ritual.

The elements also influence the celebration of the Wheel of the Year—a series of eight festivals marking the changing seasons and agricultural cycles. Each of these festivals is associated with specific elemental energies that reflect the natural world's rhythms. For example, the festival of Imbolc, celebrated in early February, is often linked to the element of Fire, representing the growing strength of the Sun and the quickening of life within the Earth. Beltane, celebrated in May, is associated with both Fire and Water, symbolizing the passionate energies of love and fertility.

As Wiccans move through the Wheel of the Year, they attune themselves to the changing elemental energies and incorporate corresponding rituals and symbols into their celebrations. This attunement not only deepens their connection to the natural world but also strengthens their awareness of the cyclical nature of existence and the sacredness of the seasons.

Wiccans believe that the elements are not only external forces but also internal aspects of the self. Each individual is seen as a microcosm of the natural world, containing within them the elemental energies. This belief fosters self-reflection and spiritual growth, as practitioners seek to balance and harmonize these elemental forces within themselves.

For example, if an individual finds themselves feeling scattered or unfocused, they may work with the element of Air to enhance mental clarity and communication. If they are seeking emotional healing or greater intuition, they may turn to the element of Water. By recognizing and working with the elemental energies within, Wiccans aim to bring balance and harmony to their own lives, aligning their inner selves with the forces of the natural world and the divine.

Wiccans adhere to the ethical principle known as the "Threefold Law" or the "Law of Return," which states that the energy one puts into the universe will return to them threefold. This principle emphasizes the significance of balance and responsibility in working with the elements and magick. Practitioners are encouraged to utilize magick for positive and constructive purposes, avoiding harm to others or themselves.

The elements serve as a reminder of the interconnectedness and balance that is inherent in the natural world. Wiccans recognize that the misuse or imbalance of elemental energies can have consequences, both on a personal and collective level. This recognition reinforces the ethical consideration of maintaining equilibrium and harmony in all magickal workings and spiritual practices.

In conclusion, the elements of Earth, Air, Fire, Water, and Spirit hold a profound and guiding influence in Wiccan practice, shaping rituals, magickal workings, and the spiritual journey of practitioners. These elements are not merely symbolic but are believed to be present within the practitioner and the natural world. The elements are invoked to create sacred space, imbue intentions with specific energies, and align with the cycles of the Wheel of the Year. They also serve as a means of self-reflection and spiritual growth, fostering balance and harmony within the individual. The ethical consideration of balance and responsibility in working with the elements underscores the importance of maintaining equilibrium in all magickal practices. The elements are a source of guidance, inspiration, and unity in Wicca, reinforcing the belief that all of life is sacred and interconnected, and that the divine is immanent within and around us.

CHAPTER VII

Tools of the Craft

The Athame, Wand, Chalice, and Pentacle

In the intricate tapestry of Wiccan spirituality, the tools of the trade hold a significant place. Among these tools, the athame, wand, chalice, and pentacle are revered instruments that play essential roles in rituals and magickal workings. Each of these tools carries its symbolism, energy, and purpose in Wicca, serving as conduits for directing and focusing magickal energy. In this section, we will delve into the significance and symbolism of the athame, wand, chalice, and pentacle, shedding light on their roles and importance in Wiccan practice.

The athame is a double-edged ritual knife with a straight blade, often featuring a black handle. In Wiccan practice, the athame represents the element of Fire and is linked with the will and the power of transformation. It is not used for cutting physical objects but is a symbolic and energetic tool employed to direct magickal energy. The athame is a symbol of the practitioner's will and intent, and it is used to cast and release energy, create boundaries, and draw symbols or sigils in the air or on other magickal tools.

The athame's use is typically confined to the casting and closing of the magickal circle, a fundamental practice in Wiccan rituals. By drawing the athame around the perimeter of the circle, practitioners create a sacred and protected space in which they can work magick and connect with the divine. The athame's energy is associated with the power to transform and manifest intentions, making it a potent tool for ritual precision and focus.

The wand is a cylindrical tool, traditionally made of wood and adorned with symbols and decorations. It represents the element of Air and is associated with intellect, communication, and the realm of ideas. The wand is used to channel and direct energy, and it serves as an extension of the practitioner's will and intention. It is often employed in spells and rituals that require precise energy direction or when invoking the energies of the elemental realms.

In Wiccan practice, the wand can be used to draw symbols or sigils in the air, to bless or consecrate objects, or to direct energy toward a specific goal. Its energies are linked to the power of thought and clear communication, making it a valuable tool for conveying intent during ritual workings. The wand's use reinforces the Wiccan belief in the interconnectedness of thought and manifestation, emphasizing the importance of focused intent in magickal practice.

The chalice is a ceremonial cup or goblet, often made of metal or glass, and it represents the element of Water. The chalice is associated with emotions, intuition, and the realm of feelings and dreams. It is a symbol of the divine feminine and is used to hold and consecrate liquids, such as water, wine, or herbal infusions, that are used in ritual libations.

In Wiccan rituals, the chalice is a tool of communion and connection. It is often used to share "Cakes and Ale" or "Cakes and Wine," a ritual act where participants partake of food and drink as a symbol of sharing in the divine and fostering a sense of community. The chalice's energies are aligned with the nurturing and purifying qualities of Water, and it acts as a reminder of the importance of honoring one's emotions and intuition in spiritual practice. It is a symbol of the sacredness of the physical world and the interconnectedness of all life.

The pentacle, or pentagram, is known as a five-pointed star within a circle, often made of metal, wood, or stone. It represents the element of Earth and embodies the concept of unity and elemental balance. Each of the five points of the star corresponds to one of the elements—Earth, Air, Fire, Water, and Spirit—and the circle symbolizes the interconnectedness and harmony of these elemental forces.

In Wiccan practice, the pentacle is used as a symbol of protection, balance, and manifestation. It is often placed on an altar or within the magickal circle to align with the elemental energies and to serve as a focal point for ritual workings. The pentacle reinforces the belief that all of life is sacred and interconnected, and it acts as a reminder of the importance of maintaining balance and harmony in all magickal practices. It is a symbol of the divine presence that resides within all things and the unity of the physical and spiritual realms.

In Wiccan rituals, the athame, wand, chalice, and pentacle are often used together to create a sacred and focused space. The casting of the circle, performed with the athame, defines the ritual area and serves as a protective barrier. The wand is used to direct energy and intention, often in the form of drawing symbols or invoking elemental energies. The chalice holds the sacred liquid, representing the element of Water and symbolizing the shared communion with the divine. The pentacle, placed on the altar, serves as a representation of the interconnected elements and a focal point for magickal workings.

These tools are consecrated and charged with energy before each ritual, aligning them with the practitioner's intent and the energies of the elements. Their use in rituals reinforces the Wiccan belief in the power of focused intent and symbolism. Through these tools, practitioners create a sacred and harmonious space where they can work magick, connect with the divine, and seek spiritual growth.

Wiccans approach the use of these tools with a strong ethical foundation, guided by principles such as the "Threefold Law" or the "Law of Return." This ethical framework emphasizes the responsibility of practitioners to use magick and ritual for positive and constructive purposes, avoiding harm to others or oneself. The tools serve as reminders of the interconnectedness and balance that are inherent in the natural world, reinforcing the importance of maintaining equilibrium in all magickal practices.

In conclusion, the athame, wand, chalice, and pentacle are cherished and potent tools of magick in Wiccan practice, each carrying its symbolism, energy, and purpose. These tools are used to create sacred space, channel and direct energy, and foster communion with

the
divine. Their use reinforces the Wiccan belief in focused intent, symbolism, and the interconnectedness of all life. Ethical considerations guide practitioners in the responsible and constructive use of these tools, ensuring that their magickal practices are in harmony with the principles of balance and unity that are central to Wiccan spirituality. The athame, wand, chalice, and pentacle are not merely instruments; they are embodiments of the sacred and powerful forces that shape the Wiccan spiritual journey.

The Book of Shadows

In the realm of Wiccan spirituality, the Book of Shadows stands as one of the most revered and mysterious elements of the craft. This ancient and sacred tome serves as a personal grimoire, containing a practitioner's rituals, spells, incantations, correspondences, and insights. The Book of Shadows, often abbreviated as BoS, is not only a repository of magickal knowledge but a reflection of a Wiccan's spiritual journey. In this section, we will delve into the significance, history, and evolving nature of the Book of Shadows, shedding light on its roles and importance in contemporary Wiccan practice.

The term "Book of Shadows" has been associated with Wicca for decades, but its origin remains a topic of debate among scholars as well as practitioners. One prevailing theory suggests that the name originated from a mistranslation of an Italian term, possibly "libro delle ombre" or "libro degli ombre," which translates to "book of shadows" or "book of shade." Another theory suggests that it may be a reference to the secrecy and hidden nature of the book, as it contains the hidden knowledge of the craft.

Regardless of its origin, the name "Book of Shadows" has become synonymous with the Wiccan grimoire, representing the mystical and magickal aspects of the craft. The book's name signifies its role as a repository of esoteric knowledge, rituals, and practices that are often kept in the shadows, away from the prying eyes of the uninitiated.

The roots of the Book of Shadows can be traced back to an array of historical sources, including medieval grimoires, folklore, and the practices of cunning folk. It was during the mid-20th century that Gerald Gardner, often considered the father of modern Wicca, introduced the concept of the Book of Shadows as it is known today. Gardner claimed that he had obtained a Book of Shadows from his initiate, Dorothy Clutterbuck, and that this grimoire formed the basis of his Wiccan tradition.

Gardner's Book of Shadows contained rituals, spells, correspondences, and lore that he had collected and adapted from various sources, including the practices of the New Forest coven and Aleister Crowley's ceremonial magick. It served as a foundational text for Gardnerian Wicca and was handed down from High Priestess to High Priestess. Gardner's Book of Shadows laid the groundwork for the development of other Wiccan traditions, each of which created its own unique version of the grimoire.

As Wicca spread and diversified in the latter half of the 20th century, so too did the Book of Shadows. Many Wiccans and Wiccan traditions developed their own versions of the book, adapting and expanding upon the material in accordance with their beliefs and practices. This evolution has led to a wide variety of Books of Shadows, each reflecting the unique spiritual journey and experiences of its creator.

The Book of Shadows serves several essential roles in Wiccan practice. Firstly, it is a repository of knowledge, containing information on rituals, spells, correspondences, and herbal and magickal lore. Practitioners use it as a reference guide for conducting rituals, casting spells, and understanding the symbolism and correspondences associated with different elements, deities, and phases of the moon.

Secondly, the Book of Shadows serves as a record of one's personal spiritual journey. Many Wiccans include journal entries, dreams, insights, and reflections in their grimoires. This allows them to track their growth, experiences, and evolving understanding of the craft over time. It becomes a living document that reflects the practitioner's spiritual evolution.

Thirdly, the Book of Shadows is a tool for passing down Wiccan traditions and practices. In some covens and traditions, it is customary for the High Priestess or High Priest to copy the Book of Shadows for each initiate, ensuring that the knowledge and rituals are preserved and passed on to the next generation of practitioners. This tradition of creating and sharing a Book of Shadows continues to be a vital aspect of many Wiccan traditions.

One of the defining features of the Book of Shadows is its personalization. Each practitioner's grimoire is unique and reflects their individual experiences, beliefs, and practices. While there may be common elements shared among various Books of Shadows, such as the Wiccan Rede or the Charge of the Goddess, the specifics of rituals, spells, and correspondences are often tailored to the practitioner's tradition and personal preferences.

The act of creating one's Book of Shadows is a deeply personal and magickal process. Many Wiccans take great care in handcrafting their grimoires, choosing materials, illustrations, and calligraphy that resonate with their spiritual path. This personalization not only imbues the book with the practitioner's energy but also enhances their connection to the rituals and practices contained within.

The Book of Shadows has historically been shrouded in secrecy, with access restricted to initiates and members of a coven. This secrecy served several purposes, including the protection of the craft from persecution and the preservation of the sacred and esoteric knowledge contained within the book.

In some Wiccan traditions, access to the Book of Shadows is granted only to initiates who have undergone a period of training and initiation. This process ensures that the knowledge and practices are passed down in a responsible and respectful manner. However, in contemporary Wicca, there has been a shift toward greater transparency and accessibility. Many Wiccans now share their Book of Shadows with a broader audience, whether through published works or online resources, while still respecting the tradition's core principles and ethical considerations.

Wiccans approach the Book of Shadows with a strong ethical foundation, guided by principles such as the "Threefold Law" or the "Law of Return." This ethical framework emphasizes the responsibility of practitioners to use magick and ritual for positive and constructive purposes, avoiding harm to others or themselves. The Book of Shadows is a tool for empowerment, personal growth, and spiritual development, and its contents should reflect these principles.

In conclusion, the Book of Shadows stands as a cherished and mysterious aspect of Wiccan spirituality. It serves as a repository of magickal knowledge, a record of one's spiritual journey, and a tool for passing down Wiccan traditions and practices. The book's evolution reflects the diversity and adaptability of Wicca as a contemporary spiritual path. Its personalization and individuality are central to its role, as each practitioner's grimoire is a reflection of their unique experiences and beliefs. The Book of Shadows, shrouded in secrecy and tradition, continues to be a source of inspiration, empowerment, and connection for Wiccans, while ethical considerations guide its use in a responsible and constructive manner.

Using Tools in Ritual and Magick

Wicca, known as a modern pagan, witchcraft religion, has gained significant popularity over the past century. Central to Wiccan practices are rituals and magick, both of which play crucial roles in connecting practitioners to the spiritual world and harnessing the energies of the universe. Tools are fundamental elements in Wiccan rituals and magick, serving as conduits for channeling intention and energy. These tools, imbued with symbolism and significance, are essential in Wicca, as they aid practitioners in focusing their intentions and connecting with the divine. In this section, we will explore the importance of using tools in ritual and magick in Wicca, examining their roles, symbolism, and how they contribute to the spiritual journey of a Wiccan practitioner.

Wiccan rituals are intricate ceremonies that celebrate the cycles of nature, honor deities, and invoke magical energies. These rituals often involve the use of various tools, each with its unique purpose. The most iconic and central of these tools is the athame, a ritual dagger with a double-edged blade. The athame represents the element of fire and is used to direct and channel energy in rituals. It is not intended for physical cutting, but rather for drawing symbols, casting circles, and directing the practitioner's will. The athame, when consecrated and charged, becomes a potent symbol of power and authority in Wiccan rituals, serving as an extension of the practitioner's intent and energy.

Another essential tool in Wiccan practice is the chalice or goblet, representing the element of water. This vessel is used for holding and consecrating liquids, typically wine or water, which are blessed and shared during rituals. The chalice symbolizes the feminine aspect of divinity and the receptive qualities of water, promoting the balance of energies within the ritual space. It is often paired with the athame in the symbolic Great Rite, a ritualistic representation of the union of the god and goddess, and the creation of life.

Wands, representing the element of air, are also fundamental tools in Wiccan practice. Typically made from wood, wands are used for directing energy and intention in a ritual. A wand is seen as an extension of the practitioner's willpower, allowing them to cast circles, invoke spirits, or channel energy. It is through the wand that the practitioner can connect with the airy qualities of thought, communication, and intellect, aligning their intent with the powers of the mind.

The pentacle, representing the element of earth, is a flat, disk-shaped object often made of metal or wood, engraved with a five-pointed star surrounded by a circle. It symbolizes the material world and the connection between the spiritual and physical realms. The pentacle is used to consecrate and bless objects, as well as to invoke the energies of the earth during rituals. It serves as a reminder of the importance of grounding and staying connected to the natural world, aligning practitioners with the energies of the earth.

Candles, incense, and crystals are also common tools in Wiccan rituals and magick. Candles symbolize the element of fire and are used to represent the presence of the divine, as well as to set the mood and create a sacred atmosphere. Different colored candles are often chosen for specific intentions, such as love, healing, or protection. Incense, representing air, serves to purify and cleanse the ritual space, as well as to aid in meditation and concentration. Crystals, associated with various elements depending on their composition, are used for their vibrational energies and healing properties, enhancing the power of spells and rituals.

The use of tools in Wiccan rituals and magick extends beyond their elemental associations. Each tool is carefully chosen, consecrated, and charged by the practitioner to attune it to their specific magical intent. This process infuses the tools with the practitioner's energy and intention, making them powerful instruments for manifesting their desires and connecting with the divine. Additionally, many tools are passed down through lineages or covens, further imbuing them with the energy and wisdom of previous practitioners.

Symbolism is a crucial aspect of Wiccan practice, and tools are rich in symbolism that resonates with the practitioner's spiritual journey. For example, the athame's dual blade represents the duality of nature, the God and Goddess, and the balance of opposites. The chalice illustrates the womb of the Goddess and the divine feminine, emphasizing the importance of nurturing and receptivity in Wiccan spirituality. Wands, with their phallic shape, represent the masculine divine and the creative force of willpower. The pentacle's five points represent the elements and the spirit, encompassed by the circle, symbolizing the unity of all aspects of existence.

In Wicca, tools are not seen as mere physical objects but as extensions of the practitioner's spiritual self. They serve as points of focus, helping to direct energy and intention towards a specific goal or outcome. By incorporating tools into their rituals and magick, practitioners create a tangible and symbolic link between the mundane and the sacred, allowing them to tap into the transformative powers of the universe.

The use of tools in Wiccan rituals and magick also contributes to the practitioner's spiritual growth and development. As they work with these tools, they develop a deeper understanding of symbolism, energy manipulation, and the interconnectedness of all things. Each tool becomes a teacher, guiding the practitioner on their spiritual journey and helping them establish their magical abilities. This process of learning and growth is an integral part of Wiccan practice, as it encourages self-discovery and personal empowerment.

Furthermore, the use of tools in Wiccan rituals and magick fosters a sense of connection and continuity with the traditions of the past. Many Wiccans draw inspiration from the practices of their ancestors and seek to honor the wisdom and knowledge of those who came before them. By using tools that have been passed down through generations, practitioners can tap into the collective energy and wisdom of their lineage, strengthening their connection to their spiritual roots.

In conclusion, tools are indispensable in Wiccan rituals and magick, serving as conduits for intention, symbolism, and spiritual growth. These carefully chosen and consecrated objects represent the elements, embody symbolism, and empower practitioners to connect with the divine and manifest their desires. Through the use of tools, Wiccans create a bridge between the physical as well as the spiritual realms, fostering personal growth and a sense of continuity with the past. As Wicca continues to evolve and adapt, the use of tools remains a vital and cherished aspect of this vibrant and diverse spiritual tradition.

CHAPTER VIII

Wiccan Symbols and Their Meanings

The Pentacle

The pentacle is a quintessential symbol in Wicca, known as a modern pagan, witchcraft religion that celebrates nature, spirituality, and the interconnectedness of all things. It holds a central and revered place within Wiccan practices, serving as a powerful tool and symbol that embodies a range of meanings and purposes. In this section, we will delve into the significance of the pentacle in Wicca, exploring its history, symbolism, usage, and its role in connecting Wiccans with the spiritual world and the natural elements.

Historically, the pentacle has roots in various cultures and traditions, predating its association with Wicca. It can be tracked down to ancient civilizations such as Mesopotamia and ancient Greece, where it was used as a symbol of protection, harmony, and the five elements: earth, air, fire, water, and spirit. In Wicca, the pentacle has been adopted and adapted, infused with its unique symbolism and meanings, making it a cornerstone of the religion. One of the primary roles of the pentacle in Wicca is to represent the element of earth. Each of the five points of the pentacle corresponds to one of the elements, with the bottom point symbolizing earth. This elemental connection is significant in Wiccan rituals and magick, where practitioners seek to harmonize with and harness the energies of the natural world. By using the pentacle, Wiccans can invoke the grounding and stabilizing properties of earth, fostering a deeper connection to the physical realm and the cycles of nature.

Moreover, the pentacle is often used as a tool for consecration and purification in Wiccan rituals. Before conducting a ritual or spell, practitioners may pass objects through the pentacle to cleanse and bless them. This process assists to remove any negative energies or influences, ensuring that only pure and positive energies are present in the ritual space. The pentacle acts as a gateway between the mundane and the sacred, purifying objects and imbuing them with spiritual significance.

In addition to its elemental and purifying roles, the pentacle holds deep symbolic meaning within Wicca. It is often seen as a representation of the pentagram, a five-pointed star enclosed within a circle. The pentagram symbolizes the balance and harmony of the elements, with each point corresponding to one of the five elements. The circle around the pentagram represents the interconnectedness of these elements and the unity of all aspects of existence. This symbolism aligns with the core beliefs of Wicca, emphasizing the importance of balance, harmony, and the cyclical nature of life and death.

Furthermore, the pentacle is associated with protection and warding off negative energies or entities. Wiccans often use it as a talisman, amulet, or as part of their altar setup to create a protective barrier around themselves or their sacred space. The pentacle's symbolism of balance and unity is believed to help maintain a sense of equilibrium and keep harmful energies at bay, ensuring a safe and spiritually conducive environment for rituals and spellwork.

The pentacle also plays a significant role in Wiccan jewelry and personal adornment. Many Wiccans wear pentacle necklaces or rings as a symbol of their faith and as a constant reminder of their spiritual connection to the elements and the divine. Wearing the pentacle is a way for practitioners to express their beliefs, signal their membership in the Wiccan community, and keep their connection to their faith close to their hearts, quite literally.

Moreover, the pentacle is frequently featured on Wiccan altars as an essential and symbolic tool. It is often placed in the northern quarter of the altar, representing the element of earth. The pentacle serves as a focal point during rituals, as it is where objects are consecrated, blessed, and charged with intent. By incorporating the pentacle into their altars, Wiccans create a sacred and consecrated space that allows them to connect with the spiritual world and the energies of the elements.

The pentacle's significance is not limited to its elemental associations, purification properties, and protective qualities. It also serves as a symbol of the pentacle's wearer or practitioner's devotion to Wicca and their commitment to its principles. For many Wiccans, the pentacle embodies their belief in the sacredness of nature, the unity of all things, and the importance of balance and harmony in their lives. It serves as a reminder of their spiritual path and the values they hold dear.

In conclusion, the pentacle holds a special place in Wicca, embodying a rich tapestry of meanings and purposes. From its elemental symbolism to its role in purification, protection, and personal adornment, the pentacle is a versatile and significant symbol in Wiccan practice. It represents the essence of Wicca itself, emphasizing the interconnectedness of all things, the importance of balance and harmony, and the sacredness of nature. As Wicca continues to evolve and thrive, the pentacle remains a cherished and enduring symbol that continues to inspire and empower its practitioners on their spiritual journey.

The Triple Goddess and Horned God

Wicca, a modern pagan, witchcraft religion, draws its inspiration from a varied range of historical and mythological sources. Two central figures in Wiccan spirituality are the Triple Goddess and the Horned God. These deities are revered and celebrated in Wiccan rituals and hold a prominent place within the religion's belief system. In this section, we will explore the significance of the Triple Goddess and Horned God in Wicca, delving into their symbolism, roles, and the profound influence they have on the spiritual journey of Wiccan practitioners.

The Triple Goddess is a fundamental concept in Wiccan theology, representing the three primary phases of the lunar cycle and the stages of a woman's life. She is often depicted as a maiden, mother, and crone, symbolizing youth, fertility, and wisdom, respectively. Each aspect of the Triple Goddess is associated with specific attributes and qualities that resonate with the natural cycles of life and the seasons. The maiden represents new beginnings, growth, and the waxing moon. She embodies innocence, enthusiasm, and the promise of the future. The mother, associated with the full moon, represents nurturing, fertility, and abundance. She is a symbol of creativity, compassion, and the peak of life's energy. The crone, aligned with the waning moon, represents wisdom, transformation, and the cycles of death and rebirth. She embodies introspection, experience, and the passage into the next phase of existence.

The Triple Goddess is often invoked in Wiccan rituals to honor these different aspects and to connect with the cyclical nature of existence. Practitioners may call upon the maiden for new beginnings, the mother for abundance and healing, and the crone for guidance and wisdom. By working with the Triple Goddess, Wiccans seek to attune themselves to the rhythms of nature, the phases of the moon, and the cycles of life, death, and rebirth. This connection fosters a more profound understanding of the interconnectedness of all things and helps practitioners align their spiritual journey with the natural world.

The Horned God, the counterpart to the Triple Goddess, is another key figure in Wiccan spirituality. Often depicted as a stag or a man with antlers, the Horned God symbolizes the masculine divine and the wild, untamed aspects of nature. He represents the life force, virility, and the cycles of the seasons. The Horned God is associated with the sun, and his energy is strongest during the warmer months when nature is in full bloom. He embodies strength, courage, and the power of transformation.

The Horned God is often invoked in Wiccan rituals that celebrate the cycles of nature, such as the sabbats. During the sabbats, which mark the solstices, equinoxes, and other significant points in the natural calendar, Wiccans honor the Horned God as the embodiment of the sun's energy and the vitality of the Earth. He is the consort and partner of the Triple Goddess, and their union symbolizes the balance of masculine and the feminine energies in the universe. This union is often celebrated symbolically through the Great Rite, a ritualistic representation of the sacred union of the god and goddess.

One of the key aspects of the Horned God is his connection to the wilderness and the animal kingdom. He is often referred to as the Lord of the Animals, and his antlers symbolize his affinity with the stag and the forest. Wiccans who work with the Horned God may seek his guidance in matters of strength, courage, and the primal aspects of human nature. His energy can be a source of inspiration for personal transformation and spiritual growth.

The Triple Goddess and the Horned God are not only revered as deities but also as archetypes that represent universal concepts and energies. They serve as symbols of the duality and balance that is central to Wiccan spirituality. The duality of the Triple Goddess and Horned God reflects the interplay of light and dark, life and death, and the changing seasons. This duality is not limited to gender but encompasses all aspects of existence, emphasizing the importance of balance and harmony in the Wiccan worldview.

Moreover, the Triple Goddess and Horned God are seen as immanent deities, meaning that they are present in the natural world and within each individual. Wiccans believe that these deities can be experienced directly through nature, meditation, and rituals. By connecting with the Triple Goddess and the Horned God, practitioners can tap into their energies and qualities, drawing inspiration and guidance from these divine archetypes.

In conclusion, the Triple Goddess and Horned God are central figures in Wicca, representing the duality and balance that underlie the religion's belief system. The Triple Goddess embodies the phases of the moon and the cycles of life, while the Horned God represents the masculine divine and the vitality of the Earth. Together, they symbolize the interconnectedness of all things and the harmony of nature. By working with these archetypes, Wiccans seek to align themselves with the rhythms of the natural world, fostering a deeper connection to the cycles of life, death, and rebirth, and embracing the duality and balance that are at the heart of Wiccan spirituality.

Other Common Symbols and Their Significance

Wicca, a modern pagan, witchcraft religion, is rich in symbolism and draws from a variety of sources, including ancient traditions, folklore, and mythology. Symbols play a crucial role in Wiccan rituals, spells, and practices, serving as powerful tools for focusing intention, connecting with the spiritual world, and conveying deeper meanings. In addition to the Triple Goddess and the

Horned God, several other symbols hold significance within Wicca, each representing unique aspects of the religion's beliefs and practices. In this section, we will explore some of these common symbols and delve into their meanings and roles in Wiccan spirituality.

The pentacle, which we have discussed earlier in the context of the Triple Goddess and Horned God, is one of the most recognizable symbols in Wicca. It consists of a five-pointed star enclosed within a circle and symbolizes the elements of earth, air, fire, water, and spirit. The pentacle serves as a powerful tool for consecration and protection, as well as a representation of the interconnectedness of the elements and the unity of all things. Wiccans often use the pentacle in their rituals and spellwork to invoke the elemental energies and to create a sacred space that is in harmony with the natural world.

The cauldron is another symbol commonly associated with Wicca. It represents the feminine divine, the womb of the goddess, and the transformative power of the elements. The cauldron is often used in Wiccan rituals for mixing herbs, oils, and other ingredients, symbolizing the blending of energies and intentions. It is also seen as a vessel of rebirth and regeneration, as it is believed to symbolize the goddess's cauldron of transformation, where souls are purified and renewed. In this context, the cauldron serves as a symbol of spiritual growth and evolution.

The broomstick, often known as a besom in Wiccan circles, is a symbol of purification and cleansing. In traditional witchcraft, brooms were used to sweep away negative energies from the home and ritual space. In Wicca, the besom is often used in rituals to symbolically sweep away negative influences, allowing for a clean slate and a purified environment. It is also associated with flying, a common theme in witchcraft folklore, symbolizing the ability to transcend mundane limitations and journey to the realms of the spirit.

The wand is a tool of magical significance in Wicca and is often used to direct and channel energy. Wands are typically made from wood and can be adorned with crystals, gemstones, or other symbols. The wand represents the element of air and the power of the mind and intention. It is seen as an extension of the practitioner's willpower, allowing them to cast circles, invoke spirits, or channel energy for specific purposes. The wand serves as a tool for focusing and directing energy in rituals and spellwork.

Candles hold a prominent place in Wiccan rituals and are used to represent the element of fire. They symbolize illumination, transformation, and the presence of the divine. Different colored candles are often chosen for specific intentions, such as red for love, green for healing, or white for purification. Lighting candles in rituals not only creates a sacred atmosphere but also serves as a means of focusing intention and connecting with the spiritual world. Candle magic, a form of spellwork involving candles, is a common practice in Wicca and harnesses the energy of fire to manifest desired outcomes.

The athame, a ritual dagger with a double-edged blade, is another essential tool in Wicca. It represents the element of fire and is used for directing and channeling energy in rituals. The athame is not intended for physical cutting but is rather used for drawing symbols, casting circles, and directing the practitioner's will. When consecrated and charged, the athame becomes a potent symbol of power and authority in Wiccan rituals, serving as an extension of the practitioner's intent and energy.

Lastly, the moon, particularly the phases of the moon, holds immense significance in Wicca. The lunar cycle, which includes the new moon, waxing moon, full moon, and waning moon, corresponds to various aspects of the Triple Goddess and the natural cycles of life. Many Wiccan rituals and spells are timed to coincide with specific lunar phases, as they are believed to enhance the effectiveness of the magic performed. The full moon, in particular, is a time of heightened energy and is often used for rituals that involve divination, healing, and empowerment.

In conclusion, Wicca is a religion rich in symbolism, and its practitioners use various symbols to connect with the spiritual world, focus intention, and convey deeper meanings. These symbols, including the pentacle, cauldron, broomstick, wand, candles, athame, and the phases of the moon, play crucial roles in Wiccan rituals and spellwork. They represent the elements, the cycles of nature, and the interplay of light and dark, adding depth and significance to the practice of Wicca. As Wiccans continue to explore and adapt their spiritual traditions, these symbols remain a vital part of their magical and ritualistic expressions, serving as potent tools for personal growth and spiritual connection.

CHAPTER IX

Wiccan Morality and Decision-Making

Ethical Dilemmas in Everyday Life

Wicca, a modern pagan, witchcraft religion, places a strong emphasis on ethical and moral principles that guide its practitioners in their daily lives. Central to Wiccan ethics is the belief in the "Wiccan Rede," a succinct ethical guideline that states, "An it harm none, do what ye will." This principle encourages Wiccans to act responsibly, respect the free will of others, and make choices that do not cause harm to themselves or others. However, as with any belief system, the application of ethical principles in everyday life can give rise to complex and nuanced dilemmas. In this section, we will explore some of the ethical dilemmas that Wiccans may encounter in their daily lives and how they navigate these challenges while adhering to their spiritual values.

One of the most common ethical dilemmas in Wicca revolves around the concept of personal responsibility and accountability. The Wiccan Rede encourages individuals to take responsibility for their actions and the consequences that may result. This principle requires practitioners to carefully consider the potential impact of their choices on themselves and others. However, in everyday life, situations may arise where the consequences of one's actions are not immediately clear, and individuals may find themselves facing decisions that have unforeseen outcomes.

For example, a Wiccan practitioner might face the dilemma of whether to take a new job opportunity that requires relocating to a different city. While the job could offer personal and professional growth, the decision might also disrupt established relationships, routines, and community ties. In such cases, Wiccans may use divination or meditation to gain insight into the potential consequences of their choices, seeking guidance from their spiritual practice to make a decision that aligns with their values and minimizes harm to themselves and others.

Another ethical dilemma in Wicca concerns the practice of magick and spellwork. Wiccans believe in the power of intention and energy manipulation, and they use spells to achieve specific goals or desires. However, ethical questions can arise when considering the boundaries of what is considered acceptable in spellwork. For instance, a practitioner may wish to perform a spell to influence someone's actions or feelings in their favor, such as casting a love spell on a person they desire. This raises questions about consent and free will, as it may involve manipulating the thoughts or emotions of another individual.

To navigate such ethical dilemmas, many Wiccans adhere to the principle of "harm none" and refrain from using magick to interfere with the free will of others. Instead, they focus on spells that promote healing, personal growth, protection, and positive energy. Ethical considerations in spellwork emphasize the importance of respecting the autonomy and choices of individuals, even when pursuing personal desires or goals.

Environmental ethics are also a significant aspect of Wiccan spirituality, as practitioners hold a deep reverence for nature and the natural world. Ethical dilemmas related to the environment can arise when individuals are faced with choices that impact the ecosystem or the well-being of other living beings. For example, a Wiccan practitioner may encounter a situation where their profession involves activities that harm the environment, such as working in the logging or mining industry.

In such cases, Wiccans may grapple with the conflict between their livelihood and their commitment to environmental preservation. Some may choose to seek alternative employment that aligns with their ecological values, while others may strive to minimize harm within their existing roles. Environmental dilemmas underscore the importance of finding ways to live in harmony with the Earth and make choices that support the principles of sustainability and respect for the natural world.

Another ethical concern that can arise in everyday life for Wiccans is the issue of religious discrimination or intolerance. Despite the growing acceptance of diverse spiritual practices, Wiccans and other pagan traditions still face prejudice and misunderstanding in some communities. This can lead to dilemmas when Wiccans must decide whether to openly disclose their beliefs or keep them private to avoid potential discrimination. Wiccans often grapple with questions about when and how to assert their religious identity, especially in situations where they face bias or negative stereotypes. Some may choose to be open about their beliefs to educate others and promote tolerance, while others may opt for a more private approach to avoid potential conflicts. Balancing the desire for authenticity with concerns about social acceptance and discrimination is an ongoing ethical challenge for many Wiccans.

In conclusion, Wicca places a strong emphasis on ethical principles, primarily encapsulated in the Wiccan Rede: "An it harm none, do what ye will." While this guideline provides a clear moral framework for Wiccans, ethical dilemmas can still arise in everyday life. These dilemmas often revolve around issues of personal responsibility, the use of magick, environmental ethics, and religious discrimination. Wiccans navigate these challenges by seeking guidance from their spiritual practice, emphasizing harm reduction, and striving to align their actions with their values. Ultimately, the ethical dilemmas in everyday life serve as opportunities for Wiccans to deepen their understanding of their spiritual path and grow in their commitment to living ethically and responsibly in the world.

Applying Wiccan Ethics to Decision-Making

Wicca, a modern pagan, witchcraft religion, is rooted in a set of ethical principles that guide the beliefs and actions of its practitioners. Central to Wiccan ethics is the "Wiccan Rede," which succinctly states, "An it harm none, do what ye will." This principle encourages Wiccans to act responsibly, respect the free will of others, and make choices that do not cause harm to themselves or others. Applying Wiccan ethics to decision-making is a fundamental aspect of the religion, and it offers a valuable framework for navigating life's complexities. In this section, we will explore how Wiccans use their ethical principles to make decisions, drawing on their reverence for nature, personal responsibility, and respect for individual autonomy.

One of the foundational principles of Wiccan ethics is a deep reverence for nature and the interconnectedness of all living beings. This reverence extends to the environment and the belief that harming the Earth ultimately harms humanity and the spiritual balance of the world. Consequently, many Wiccans consider ecological impact when making decisions that could affect the environment. For example, when deciding on modes of transportation, they may choose options with a lower carbon footprint, such as walking, biking, or using public transport, rather than contributing to air pollution and environmental degradation. This choice aligns with their ethical commitment to minimize harm to the Earth and its ecosystems.

Personal responsibility is another core aspect of Wiccan ethics that plays a vital role in decision-making. Wiccans believe in being accountable for their actions and choices, recognizing that every decision has consequences that ripple through their lives and the lives of others. When faced with decisions, Wiccans often engage in self-reflection and consider how their choices may impact themselves, their community, and the world at large. They take responsibility for their actions and strive to make choices that are aligned with their values and the ethical guidelines of the Wiccan Rede. This sense of personal responsibility helps Wiccans make decisions that are ethical and in harmony with their spiritual beliefs.

Respect for individual autonomy and free will is a central component of the Wiccan Rede. Wiccans hold that individuals have the right to make their own choices and decisions, provided that those choices do not cause harm to others. This respect for autonomy extends to relationships, where consent and boundaries are highly valued. When Wiccans encounter situations that involve others' choices or actions, they carefully consider the importance of free will and seek to honor individual autonomy. For example, in matters of love and relationships, Wiccans may cast spells to attract love or enhance existing connections, but they are careful not to manipulate the feelings or decisions of others. Instead, they focus on self-improvement, personal growth, and creating an inviting energy that may attract like-minded individuals who share mutual interests and desires.

In addition to personal relationships, the principle of respect for free will is also applied in broader societal contexts. Wiccans may participate in social and political activism to advocate for social justice and human rights, but they do so with a commitment to respecting the autonomy and choices of others, even when advocating for change. This approach highlights their belief in the importance of balance and harmony and their dedication to ethical decision-making in all aspects of life.

Ethical decision-making in Wicca often involves considering the potential consequences of one's actions and choices. Wiccans believe that every action, whether mundane or magical, carries energetic repercussions that can affect the practitioner and the world around them. To make ethical decisions, Wiccans may engage in divination or meditation to gain insight into the potential outcomes of their choices. Divination tools including, tarot cards, runes, or scrying can provide guidance and reveal potential consequences that may not be immediately apparent. By seeking such guidance, Wiccans ensure that their decisions are well-informed and aligned with their ethical principles.

Furthermore, Wiccans emphasize the importance of mindfulness and intentionality in decision-making. Before taking action or making a choice, practitioners often engage in meditation or ritual to clarify their intentions and align them with their ethical values. This process allows them to assess whether their motivations are pure and whether their actions are in harmony with the Wiccan Rede. By approaching decision-making with mindfulness, Wiccans ensure that they are acting with a clear ethical purpose and minimizing the potential for harm.

In conclusion, Wicca's ethical principles, encapsulated in the Wiccan Rede, provide a valuable framework for decision-making that promotes responsibility, respect for free will, and harmony with nature. Wiccans apply these principles to their everyday choices, whether they relate to personal relationships, environmental impact, or social activism. By taking into account the potential consequences of their actions, respecting individual autonomy, and practicing mindfulness and intentionality,

Wiccans strive to make ethical decisions that align with their spiritual beliefs and foster a sense of responsibility to themselves, their communities, and the Earth. In doing so, they embody the core values of Wiccan ethics and contribute to a more harmonious and ethically conscious world.

CHAPTER X

The Wiccan Community and Its Values

Covens and Solitary Practitioners

Wicca, a modern pagan, witchcraft religion, offers practitioners various approaches to their spiritual journey, with two primary paths being the practice within a coven or as a solitary practitioner. Each path comes with its own set of advantages, challenges, and dynamics, catering to the different preferences and needs of individuals within the Wiccan community. In this section, we will explore the roles of covens and solitary practitioners in Wicca, examining the differences, benefits, and challenges associated with each path, and how they contribute to the diversity and vibrancy of the Wiccan tradition.

A coven is a group of Wiccan practitioners who come together to practice rituals, share knowledge, and engage in spiritual exploration as a collective. Covens vary in size, structure, and tradition, but they typically have a hierarchical system with a High Priestess and/or High Priest leading the group. Covens offer a sense of community, mentorship, and shared experience that can be immensely rewarding for practitioners. They provide opportunities for learning from experienced witches, participating in group rituals, and celebrating the sabbats and esbats with like-minded individuals.

One of the primary benefits of belonging to a coven is the sense of belonging and support it provides. Wicca can be a solitary and deeply personal spiritual path, and joining a coven offers a sense of community and camaraderie that can be comforting and fulfilling. Covens often function as a support network, offering emotional and practical assistance to members in times of need. This sense of belonging can be particularly valuable for individuals who may have felt isolated or marginalized in other aspects of their lives.

Covens also provide a structured environment for learning and growth. New practitioners can benefit from the guidance and mentorship of more experienced members, who can help them navigate the complexities of Wiccan practice, spellwork, and ritual. This mentorship fosters a sense of tradition and lineage, as knowledge is passed down from one generation of practitioners to the next. The structured and organized nature of covens can help individuals deepen their understanding of Wicca and develop their magical skills.

Moreover, group rituals within a coven can be powerful and transformative experiences. The collective energy generated during these rituals can enhance the efficacy of spellwork and allow practitioners to connect more deeply with the divine and the natural world. Group rituals also provide opportunities for communal celebrations of the sabbats and esbats, reinforcing the cyclical and seasonal aspects of Wiccan spirituality. The shared experience of these rituals can create a sense of unity and connection among coven members.

However, being part of a coven is challenging. Covens often have rules, hierarchies, and traditions that members are expected to adhere to, and these structures may not resonate with everyone. Some individuals may find that the expectations and responsibilities within a coven are restrictive or do not align with their personal beliefs or spiritual journey. Conflicts and personality clashes can arise within a coven, as in any group, potentially causing tension and discord.

In contrast to covens, solitary practitioners in Wicca walk their spiritual path independently, without the formal structure and community of a coven. Solitary Wiccans often design their own rituals, set their schedules, and choose the elements of Wiccan practice that resonate most with them. This approach offers a high degree of autonomy and flexibility, allowing individuals to tailor their spiritual journey to their unique preferences and needs.

One of the key advantages of solitary practice is the freedom it affords practitioners to explore their spirituality on their own terms. Solitary Wiccans are not bound by the rules or traditions of a coven, giving them the creative space to develop their own rituals and beliefs. This flexibility allows for a highly personalized and individualized spiritual experience, where practitioners can focus on what speaks most profoundly to them and their unique path.

Solitary practice can also be particularly well-suited to those who value privacy and introspection. It offers a degree of anonymity and independence that may be appealing to individuals who prefer to keep their spiritual beliefs and practices private. Solitary practitioners have the freedom to work in solitude, free from the scrutiny or expectations of a group, and can explore their spirituality in a way that aligns with their personal comfort levels. However, solitary practice is not without its challenges. Many individuals who follow this path face a lack of structured guidance and mentorship, which can be a hindrance, especially for newcomers to Wicca. Without the guidance of experienced practitioners, solitary Wiccans may struggle to navigate the complexities of the religion, leading to potential misconceptions or incomplete understandings of Wiccan practices and traditions.

Additionally, solitary practitioners may miss out on the sense of community and shared experience of belonging to a coven. The absence of group rituals and celebrations can be isolating, and some solitary Wiccans may find it challenging to generate the same level of energy and connection during solitary rituals. The sense of belonging and camaraderie that covens provide may be absent in solitary practice.

In conclusion, Wicca offers practitioners two distinct paths: the practice within a coven or as a solitary practitioner. Each path has its unique advantages and challenges, catering to different preferences and needs within the Wiccan community. Covens offer a sense of community, mentorship, and structured rituals, while solitary practice provides autonomy, flexibility, and personalized spirituality. The diversity of approaches within Wicca contributes to the richness and vitality of the tradition, allowing individuals to choose the path that resonates most deeply with their beliefs and spiritual journey. Ultimately, whether practicing within a coven or as a solitary, Wiccans share a commitment to the ethical principles and reverence for nature that form the core of their spirituality.

The Importance of Community

Wicca, a modern pagan, witchcraft religion, significantly emphasizes the importance of community within its spiritual practice and traditions. While Wiccan beliefs and practices can be deeply personal and individualized, the sense of belonging to a community of like-minded individuals is a vital aspect of Wiccan spirituality. In this section, we will explore the role and significance of community in Wicca, how it contributes to practitioners' spiritual growth and well-being, and how it fosters a sense of unity and shared purpose among Wiccans.

Community in Wicca is often formed through covens, which are groups of practitioners who come together to celebrate rituals, share knowledge, and support one another on their spiritual journeys. Covens can vary in size, structure, and tradition, but they typically provide a structured and supportive environment for Wiccans to connect with one another. Within covens, there is often a hierarchical system, with a High Priestess and/or High Priest leading the group and guiding its members.

One of the most significant benefits of belonging to a Wiccan community or coven is the sense of belonging and support it offers. Wicca, like many pagan traditions, can be a solitary and individualistic path. Many Wiccans find that their beliefs and practices are not mainstream and may face misunderstandings or even prejudice from those outside their community. Being part of a Wiccan community provides a sense of acceptance and understanding that can be profoundly comforting and affirming. It allows practitioners to connect with others with similar beliefs and experiences, creating a sense of kinship and camaraderie.

Coven members often serve as a support network for one another, offering emotional and practical assistance when needed. This support system can be invaluable in times of personal crisis or when facing challenges related to one's spiritual journey. Within a coven, members often share their knowledge and experiences, providing guidance and mentorship to those who are newer to the path. This mentorship fosters a sense of tradition and lineage, as knowledge is passed down from one generation of practitioners to the next.

Another crucial role of community in Wicca is the opportunity for collective ritual and celebration. Wiccan rituals, particularly those associated with the sabbats and esbats, are often conducted in a group setting. The energy generated during group rituals can be powerful and transformative, heightening the effectiveness of spellwork and allowing practitioners to connect more deeply with the divine and the natural world. The collective experience of these rituals can create a profound sense of unity and connection among coven members, reinforcing the cyclical and seasonal aspects of Wiccan spirituality.

Moreover, the sense of community in Wicca helps individuals deepen their understanding of the religion and develop their magical skills. New practitioners can benefit from the guidance and mentorship of more experienced members, who can help them navigate the complexities of Wiccan practice, spellwork, and ritual. This structured and organized learning environment allows individuals to grow and develop their spiritual abilities in a supportive and nurturing setting.

However, being part of a Wiccan community is not without its challenges. Covens often have rules, hierarchies, and traditions that members are expected to adhere to, and these structures may not resonate with everyone. Some individuals may find that the expectations and responsibilities within a coven are restrictive or do not align with their personal beliefs or spiritual journey. Conflicts and personality clashes can arise within a coven, as in any group, potentially causing tension and discord.

For those who may not resonate with the structure and dynamics of covens, or who may not have access to a local coven, solitary practice is a viable alternative. Solitary practitioners in Wicca walk their spiritual path independently, without the formal structure and community of a coven. Solitary practice offers a high degree of autonomy and flexibility, allowing individuals to tailor their spiritual journey to their unique preferences and needs.

Despite the individualistic nature of solitary practice, the importance of community still holds true for many solitary Wiccans. Many solitary practitioners seek out online communities, forums, and social media groups to connect with like-minded individuals and share experiences. These virtual communities provide a sense of camaraderie and support that can be just as meaningful as physical coven connections. Solitary Wiccans may also participate in open rituals or gatherings when available, allowing them to experience the power of collective ritual and connect with others who share their beliefs.

In conclusion, the importance of community in Wicca cannot be overstated. Whether through covens, online communities, or gatherings, the community's sense of belonging and support is a vital aspect of Wiccan spirituality. Wiccan communities offer acceptance, mentorship, and a structured environment for learning and growth. They provide collective ritual and celebration opportunities, fostering a profound sense of unity and connection among practitioners. While solitary practice remains a valid and cherished path within Wicca, the sense of community allows individuals to share their experiences, deepen their understanding of the religion, and forge meaningful connections with others who walk the same spiritual path. Ultimately, the sense of belonging and camaraderie within the Wiccan community strengthens the bonds of shared spirituality and contributes to the richness and vitality of the tradition.

Respecting Diversity within Wicca

Wicca, a modern pagan, witchcraft religion, is known for its rich tapestry of beliefs, practices, and traditions. At its core, Wicca emphasizes the veneration of nature, the celebration of the moon's cycles, and adherence to the ethical guideline of "An it harm none, do what ye will." However, within this overarching framework exists a diverse array of beliefs, rituals, and interpretations that reflect practitioners' individuality and unique spiritual journeys. Respecting diversity within Wicca is not only a matter of tolerance but a recognition of the strength and vibrancy that different perspectives bring to the religion. In this section, we will explore the importance of embracing diversity within Wicca, its various forms, and how it enriches the spiritual tapestry of the tradition.

One of the most notable aspects of diversity within Wicca is the variety of traditions and paths that exist under the broader umbrella of the religion. Wicca is not a monolithic belief system but rather a dynamic and evolving spiritual tradition. Different Wiccan traditions, such as Gardnerian, Alexandrian, Dianic, and Eclectic Wicca, offer distinct rituals, practices, and philosophies. While all these traditions share some common elements, they also diverge in significant ways, allowing practitioners to find a path that resonates most deeply with their spiritual inclinations.

The existence of multiple traditions within Wicca is a testament to the richness of the tradition and the flexibility it offers to accommodate diverse beliefs and practices. It allows individuals to find a path aligning with their values, spiritual experiences, and cultural backgrounds. This diversity also encourages practitioners to explore and deepen their understanding of the tradition, fostering an environment of continuous learning and growth.

Beyond the diversity of traditions, Wicca also celebrates individuality and the unique spiritual journeys of practitioners. Each Wiccan may have their interpretation of Wiccan beliefs and may incorporate elements from other spiritual traditions, such as herbalism, astrology, or shamanic practices, into their Wiccan practice. This eclecticism is a testament to Wicca's fluid and adaptable nature, which encourages practitioners to follow their intuition, explore their interests, and create a personal spiritual path that reflects their individuality.

Respecting diversity within Wicca extends to recognizing and including LGBTQ+ individuals within the Wiccan community. Many Wiccans affirm the importance of gender equality and embrace non-binary and gender-diverse perspectives. The Triple Goddess and Horned God, central figures in Wiccan spirituality, are often viewed as encompassing a spectrum of gender and sexuality, allowing LGBTQ+ individuals to see themselves reflected in the divine. Moreover, some Wiccan traditions, such as Dianic Wicca, emphasize the feminine divine and celebrate the goddess in her various forms, creating a space where women and gender-diverse individuals can connect with their spirituality on their terms.

Inclusivity and respect for diversity also extend to issues of race and cultural diversity within Wicca. While Wicca has European pagan roots, it has evolved to embrace practitioners from diverse cultural backgrounds and ethnicities. Many Wiccans recognize that the spiritual connection to nature and the divine transcends cultural boundaries and that individuals from various backgrounds can find meaning and resonance within the tradition. This inclusivity encourages a richer exchange of ideas and perspectives, contributing to Wicca's diversity of beliefs and practices.

Another aspect of diversity within Wicca is the recognition of practitioners with disabilities. Wiccan spirituality often emphasizes the importance of physical and mental well-being, and many rituals involve movement, dance, or meditation. However, recognizing the diversity of abilities among practitioners, many Wiccan communities strive to be inclusive by adapting rituals and practices to accommodate individuals with disabilities. This may involve providing accessible spaces, using assistive technologies, or offering alternative ways to participate in rituals.

Respecting diversity within Wicca is not just a matter of acknowledging differences but also promoting inclusivity and equity. Wiccan communities and practitioners must actively work to create safe and welcoming spaces for individuals of all backgrounds, abilities, and identities.

This may involve addressing discrimination, bias, or exclusion issues when they arise and promoting open dialogue and education within the community.

Embracing diversity within Wicca also enriches the tradition by fostering creativity and innovation. When practitioners from diverse backgrounds come together, they bring a wealth of knowledge, experiences, and perspectives that can develop new rituals, practices, and interpretations. This diversity of ideas and approaches keeps Wicca dynamic and responsive to the evolving needs of its practitioners.

Furthermore, recognizing and celebrating diversity within Wicca strengthens the bonds of the Wiccan community. Wiccans create an atmosphere of acceptance and mutual respect by embracing the differences that make each practitioner unique. This sense of unity in diversity allows individuals to feel valued and heard within the community, fostering a more profound sense of connection and shared purpose.

In conclusion, Wicca's strength lies in its diversity, encompassing many traditions, beliefs, practices, and individual spiritual journeys. Embracing diversity within Wicca is not merely a matter of tolerance but a celebration of the richness and vibrancy that different perspectives bring to the tradition. Whether through the recognition of diverse traditions, the affirmation of LGBTQ+ and gender-diverse individuals, the inclusion of practitioners from various cultural backgrounds, or the accommodation of individuals with disabilities, Wicca's commitment to diversity promotes inclusivity, equity, and creativity within the spiritual community. By respecting and celebrating diversity, Wiccans contribute to their tradition's ongoing evolution and vitality, creating a dynamic and inclusive space for all who seek to connect with the divine and the natural world.

CHAPTER XI

Modern Interpretations and Evolving Ethics

Eclectic Wicca

Eclectic Wicca is a dynamic and diverse branch of the modern pagan, witchcraft religion known as Wicca. Unlike traditional Wiccan traditions that adhere to specific rituals and beliefs, eclectic Wicca is characterized by its openness to a wide range of spiritual practices, beliefs, and traditions. Eclectic Wiccans often draw inspiration from various sources, blending elements of different traditions and creating a unique and personalized spiritual path. In this section, we will explore the principles and practices of eclectic Wicca, its strengths, challenges, and the reasons behind its appeal to a growing number of practitioners.

At the heart of eclectic Wicca is the belief in the central tenets of Wiccan spirituality: the veneration of nature, the recognition of the divine as immanent, and the adherence to the ethical guideline of "An it harm none, do what ye will." Eclectic Wiccans share these core principles with other Wiccan traditions but differ in their approach to rituals and practices. Eclectic Wicca emphasizes individuality and creativity, allowing practitioners to design their rituals, select deities, and incorporate practices that resonate with their personal beliefs and experiences.

One of the key strengths of eclectic Wicca is its flexibility and adaptability. Eclectic Wiccans can explore and integrate elements from different traditions, whether Celtic, Norse, Egyptian, or any other spiritual path that speaks to them. This approach allows individuals to create a spiritual practice that feels authentic and meaningful to them, reflecting their unique spiritual journey. The flexibility of eclectic Wicca also accommodates individuals with diverse cultural backgrounds, allowing them to honor their heritage while practicing Wicca.

Moreover, eclectic Wicca is inclusive and open to practitioners of various gender identities, sexual orientations, abilities, and backgrounds. Many eclectic Wiccans affirm the importance of gender equality and LGBTQ+ inclusivity within their practices. The eclectic approach encourages an atmosphere of acceptance and diversity, where individuals from all walks of life can find a welcoming and non-judgmental community.

Eclectic Wicca's open-mindedness and acceptance extend to its approach to deity worship. Eclectic Wiccans may choose to work with a wide range of deities or archetypes from various pantheons, including gods and goddesses from different cultures or even non-traditional figures. This diversity of deities allows practitioners to connect with the divine in ways that resonate with their personal experiences and spiritual inclinations. Eclectic Wiccans may also invoke aspects of the divine, such as the Triple Goddess and Horned God, while incorporating other deities into their rituals and spellwork.

Eclectic Wicca emphasizes the importance of direct personal experience and intuition. Practitioners are encouraged to engage in meditation, divination, and other spiritual practices that enhance their connection with the divine and the natural world. This emphasis on inner knowing and intuition enables individuals to trust their own spiritual insights and guidance, fostering a sense of empowerment and self-awareness.

However, eclectic Wicca is not without its challenges. The freedom to blend different traditions and practices can be both a strength and a potential source of confusion. Eclectic Wiccans must navigate the delicate balance of honoring the traditions they draw from while ensuring their practice remains coherent and meaningful. The absence of strict guidelines can lead to a lack of structure and consistency in some eclectic practices, making it challenging for newcomers to understand and embrace the tradition.

Furthermore, eclectic Wiccans may encounter criticism or skepticism from practitioners of more traditional Wiccan traditions, who view eclectic practices as deviating from the established norms of the religion. This tension between eclectic and traditional Wiccan communities can sometimes lead to misunderstandings and conflicts within the larger Wiccan community.

In conclusion, eclectic Wicca is a diverse and vibrant branch of the modern pagan, witchcraft religion that emphasizes personalization, creativity, and open-mindedness. Eclectic Wiccans draw inspiration from various traditions, blend diverse elements into their practices, and create a unique and meaningful spiritual path. The flexibility and inclusivity of eclectic Wicca allow practitioners to explore their spirituality in ways that resonate with their personal beliefs and experiences. While this approach offers numerous benefits, it also presents challenges related to maintaining coherence and structure within individual practices and navigating potential tensions with more traditional Wiccan traditions. Nonetheless, eclectic Wicca continues to grow in popularity, attracting practitioners who value the freedom to craft a spirituality that reflects their unique spiritual journeys and beliefs while remaining rooted in the core principles of Wiccan spirituality.

Wicca in the 21st Century

Wicca, a modern pagan, witchcraft religion, has evolved significantly since its emergence in the mid-20th century. As we find ourselves in the 21st century, Wicca continues to adapt and grow in response to the changing cultural, social, and technological landscape. This section explores how Wicca has evolved and manifested itself in the 21st century, examining its continued relevance, challenges, and opportunities in the modern world.

One of the most notable developments in 21st-century Wicca is its increased visibility and acceptance. While Wicca and paganism were once largely marginalized and misunderstood, they have gained recognition and legitimacy in many parts of the world. This shift is partly due to Wiccan activists, authors, and organizations working to dispel misconceptions and promote understanding of the religion. Wicca is now legally recognized as a religion in several countries, granting its practitioners the same rights and protections as adherents of more mainstream religions.

The advent of the internet and social media has played a significant role in this increased visibility. Wiccans and pagans worldwide can now connect and share their beliefs, experiences, and rituals online. Websites, forums, blogs, and social media platforms have become Wiccan community and education hubs, allowing practitioners to access resources, participate in discussions, and form virtual covens or study groups. This global connectivity has helped Wiccans build a sense of community and solidarity that transcends geographical boundaries.

In the 21st century, Wicca has also embraced a more diverse and inclusive approach. While the religion was initially influenced by Western occultism and folklore, it has since incorporated elements from a wide range of cultural traditions and belief systems. Eclecticism, which allows practitioners to blend various spiritual influences into their practice, has become increasingly common. This openness to diversity has made Wicca more inclusive of practitioners from different cultural backgrounds, gender identities, sexual orientations, and abilities.

Inclusivity within Wicca extends to its approach to gender and sexuality. Many Wiccans affirm the importance of gender equality and LGBTQ+ inclusivity within their practices. The Triple Goddess and Horned God, central figures in Wiccan spirituality, are often viewed as encompassing a spectrum of gender and sexuality, allowing LGBTQ+ individuals to see themselves reflected in the divine. Some Wiccan traditions, such as Dianic Wicca, emphasize the feminine divine and celebrate the goddess in her various forms, creating a space where women and gender-diverse individuals can connect with their spirituality on their terms.

Furthermore, Wicca's connection to environmentalism and nature worship has resonated with the 21st century's growing environmental consciousness. Many Wiccans see themselves as stewards of the Earth and advocate for environmental sustainability, conservation, and ethical treatment of animals. This alignment with ecological values has made Wicca attractive to individuals who seek a spiritual path that emphasizes a deep connection to nature and the environment.

While Wicca has seen significant growth and adaptation in the 21st century, it also faces challenges and misconceptions. Some individuals still hold biased or negative stereotypes about Wicca, viewing it as a form of "devil worship" or as superstition. This ignorance can lead to prejudice, discrimination, or misunderstandings, especially in areas where Wicca is less understood or accepted.

Additionally, the commercialization and commodification of Wiccan practices and tools have raised ethical concerns within the community. Many Wiccans believe in the importance of respecting the sacredness of their practices and rituals, and the mass production and commercialization of Wiccan items can be seen as undermining the authenticity and spiritual significance of these practices.

In conclusion, in the 21st century, Wicca is a dynamic and evolving religion that has adapted to the changing times while remaining rooted in its core principles of reverence for nature, ethical behavior, and the veneration of the divine. Increased visibility, technological advancements, inclusivity, and an alignment with environmental values have all contributed to Wicca's growth and relevance in the modern world. However, challenges such as misconceptions and commercialization persist and require ongoing efforts to educate and promote understanding. As we move further into the 21st century, Wicca's continued evolution will likely be shaped by the interplay of tradition and innovation, as it continues to find its place in the diverse and interconnected global spiritual landscape.

Exploring New Ethical Challenges

Wicca, a modern pagan, witchcraft religion, is founded on a set of ethical principles encapsulated in the Wiccan Rede: "An it harm none, do what ye will." This fundamental guideline encourages practitioners to act responsibly, respect the free will of others, and make choices that do not cause harm to themselves or others. However, as Wicca continues to evolve and adapt to the changing dynamics of the 21st century, new ethical challenges have emerged that require careful consideration and exploration. In this section, we will delve into some of these emerging ethical challenges within Wicca, examining issues related to cultural appropriation, environmental responsibility, technology, and the globalization of the tradition.

One of the significant ethical challenges facing Wicca in the 21st century is the issue of cultural appropriation. As the religion has become more diverse and inclusive, practitioners have increasingly drawn inspiration from various cultural traditions and belief systems. While eclecticism and incorporating elements from multiple cultures can be enriching, they also raise questions about the appropriate and respectful use of sacred symbols, rituals, and practices from cultures that are not one's own. Wiccans must navigate the fine line between honoring and respecting diverse traditions and cultures while avoiding cultural appropriation, which can lead to the commodification or trivialization of sacred practices and beliefs.

Environmental responsibility is another pressing ethical challenge for modern Wiccans. The reverence for nature is at the core of Wiccan spirituality, and many practitioners see themselves as stewards of the Earth. However, the 21st century has brought about unprecedented environmental challenges, including climate change, habitat destruction, and species extinction. Wiccans face the ethical dilemma of aligning their spiritual beliefs with concrete actions that address these environmental crises. This challenge involves making sustainable choices in daily life, supporting eco-friendly practices, and advocating for environmental conservation and protection.

The advent of technology and the digital age has also introduced new ethical considerations for Wiccans. While the internet has provided a platform for Wiccan communities to connect, share knowledge, and build virtual covens, it has also raised issues related to privacy, misinformation, and the potential for commercialization. Practitioners must be vigilant about protecting their privacy and respecting the boundaries of others in online spaces. Additionally, the spread of misinformation and the commercialization of Wiccan practices through online marketplaces can undermine the authenticity and sacredness of the tradition, posing ethical challenges that require critical evaluation and ethical decision-making.

Globalization and the dissemination of Wicca to cultures and regions worldwide have also presented ethical dilemmas. As Wicca becomes more globalized, practitioners must consider how to honor diverse cultural perspectives and avoid imposing a Western-centric or Eurocentric view of the tradition on others. This challenge includes respecting different regions' indigenous and local spiritual traditions while fostering dialogue and understanding between practitioners from various cultural backgrounds. It also requires sensitivity to cultural nuances and differences in the interpretation and practice of Wicca.

Furthermore, issues related to representation and inclusivity have emerged as significant ethical concerns within Wicca. Practitioners recognize the importance of ensuring that the religion welcomes and includes individuals from diverse gender identities, sexual orientations, abilities, and cultural backgrounds. Wiccans must actively work to create safe and welcoming spaces within the community, challenge biases or prejudices when they arise, and promote diversity and equity within the tradition.

Wiccans often turn to their core principles and values in addressing these emerging ethical challenges, including the Wiccan Rede. The principle of "An it harm none, do what ye will" serves as a guiding light, reminding practitioners to consider the potential consequences of their actions and choices. When faced with ethical dilemmas, Wiccans engage in introspection, meditation, divination, and dialogue within their communities to arrive at ethical decisions that align with their spiritual beliefs and values.

Moreover, Wicca's emphasis on personal responsibility is crucial in addressing these ethical challenges. Practitioners recognize that every choice and action has consequences, not only in their personal lives but also in the broader world. They understand that ethical decision-making requires a sense of accountability for their impact on the environment, other individuals, and the global community.

In conclusion, like any evolving religion, Wicca faces new ethical challenges in the 21st century that require careful consideration and exploration. These challenges encompass issues of cultural appropriation, environmental responsibility, technology, globalization, representation, and inclusivity. Addressing these ethical dilemmas necessitates a commitment to the core principles of Wiccan spirituality, including the Wiccan Rede, personal responsibility, and reverence for nature. By engaging in introspection, dialogue, and ethical decision-making, Wiccans can navigate these challenges while upholding their spiritual beliefs and values in an ever-changing world.

CHAPTER XII

Living a Wiccan Life

Integrating Wiccan Values into Daily Life

Wicca, a modern pagan, witchcraft religion, is not just a set of rituals and beliefs practiced on special occasions but a way of life rooted in its core principles and values. At the heart of Wiccan spirituality is the reverence for nature, the recognition of the divine as immanent, and the adherence to the ethical guideline of "An it harm none, do what ye will." Integrating these Wiccan values into daily life is a profound and transformative practice that allows Wiccans to align their actions, decisions, and intentions with their spiritual beliefs. This section will explore how Wiccan values can be integrated into daily life, fostering a deeper connection to nature, ethical decision-making, and personal growth.

One of the fundamental principles of Wicca is the veneration of nature. Wiccans view the natural world as sacred and interconnected, recognizing the divine presence in every living being and natural element. To integrate this value into daily life, practitioners often engage in activities connecting them with nature, such as spending time outdoors, gardening, or observing the moon's cycles and seasons. These practices foster a sense of harmony and reverence for the Earth, reminding Wiccans of their role as stewards of the environment. By aligning their daily activities with the cycles of nature, Wiccans strengthen their connection to the natural world and honor the sacredness of all life.

Another core value of Wicca is the belief in the immanence of the divine. Wiccans see the divine not as distant and separate but as present within themselves and the world around them. To integrate this value into daily life, practitioners cultivate a sense of mindfulness and spiritual awareness in their everyday activities. Meditation, reflection, and moments of gratitude become essential practices that allow Wiccans to connect with the divine within themselves and in their surroundings. By recognizing the immanence of the divine, Wiccans infuse their daily lives with a sense of spiritual purpose and meaning.

The ethical guideline of "An it harm none, do what ye will" is a central tenet of Wiccan spirituality, emphasizing the importance of ethical decision-making. To integrate this value into daily life, Wiccans strive to make choices that align with the principle of harmlessness. This involves considering the potential consequences of their actions and decisions on themselves, others, and the environment. Practitioners often engage in ethical reflection and engage in discussions within their communities to understand the ethical implications of their choices better. By applying this principle in their daily lives, Wiccans seek to live by their ethical values and promote a sense of responsibility and accountability.

Wiccans also integrate their values into daily life through rituals and practices that mark significant moments and transitions. Daily rituals, such as lighting candles, offering prayers, or meditation, become opportunities to connect with the divine, set intentions, and align with Wiccan values. Celebrating the sabbats and esbats, the Wiccan festivals that mark the cycles of the moon and seasons, is another way to integrate spiritual values into daily life. These rituals allow practitioners to connect with the rhythms of nature, celebrate the changing seasons, and reflect on their spiritual journey.

Moreover, Wiccans often incorporate magical practices into their daily routines as a means of manifestation and transformation. Spells, charms, and other magical workings are performed to create positive change in their lives and the world. These practices allow Wiccans to actively engage with their values by channeling their intentions and energies toward specific goals and aspirations.

Personal growth and self-awareness are essential to integrating Wiccan values into daily life. Wiccans recognize that spiritual development is an ongoing process, and they actively work on their personal growth through self-reflection, meditation, and self-improvement practices. By aligning their actions with their values, Wiccans foster a more profound sense of self-awareness and authenticity in their daily lives, striving to live by their highest principles.

Challenges may arise when attempting to integrate Wiccan values into daily life. External pressures, societal expectations, and conflicting values can sometimes create tensions and dilemmas. Wiccans must navigate these challenges by staying true to their spiritual beliefs while also finding ways to engage in constructive dialogue and understanding with those who may hold different values.

In conclusion, integrating Wiccan values into daily life is a transformative practice that allows practitioners to align their actions, decisions, and intentions with their spiritual beliefs. By cultivating a reverence for nature, recognizing the immanence of the divine, and adhering to the ethical guideline of "An it harm none, do what ye will," Wiccans infuse their daily lives with purpose, mindfulness, and ethical awareness. Through rituals, magical practices, and self-improvement efforts, Wiccans deepen their connection to their values and foster personal growth. While challenges may arise, integrating Wiccan values ultimately leads to a life lived in harmony with nature, the divine, and one's own ethical principles, offering a profound sense of fulfillment and spiritual authenticity.

Balancing Wiccan Beliefs with Other Aspects of Life

Wicca, a modern pagan, witchcraft religion, places a strong emphasis on the integration of spiritual beliefs into daily life. Its core values, such as reverence for nature, the recognition of the immanence of the divine, and adherence to the ethical guideline of "An it harm none, do what ye will," guide Wiccans in their spiritual journey. However, like anyone following a spiritual path, Wiccans also face the challenge of balancing their beliefs with the demands of other aspects of life, such as work, family, and social responsibilities. This section explores the complexities of finding this balance, Wiccans' strategies to harmonize their beliefs with everyday life, and the benefits and challenges associated with this endeavor.

One of the key challenges in balancing Wiccan beliefs with other aspects of life is the integration of spiritual practices into daily routines. Wicca encourages regular rituals, meditation, and reflection, which require time and effort. Many practitioners find that dedicating a specific part of their day or week to their spiritual practices helps them create a sense of structure and consistency. Whether it's setting aside time for daily meditation or performing a monthly esbat ritual during the full moon, these practices become touchstones that keep Wiccans connected to their beliefs.

Wiccans also seek to infuse their daily lives with mindfulness and intentionality. This involves being present in the moment and aligning their actions with their spiritual values. For example, a simple act, like lighting a candle before a meal, can become a moment of gratitude and reflection. By infusing everyday activities with mindfulness, Wiccans bridge the gap between their spiritual beliefs and the practicalities of daily life.

Furthermore, the concept of "As above, so below; as below, so above" is central to Wiccan belief, emphasizing the interconnectedness of the spiritual and physical realms. Wiccans see the divine as immanent, meaning it exists within everything and everyone. This perspective allows them to view all aspects of life as inherently spiritual. Work, relationships, and personal growth are all opportunities to embody Wiccan values and principles. This holistic approach enables Wiccans to see their beliefs as integral to all aspects of life, rather than something separate or compartmentalized.

However, finding balance can be challenging, especially when external pressures, such as work or family responsibilities, demand significant time and attention. Wiccans often face the dilemma of wanting to dedicate more time to their spiritual practices while fulfilling their material obligations. This balancing act may require negotiation, time management, and flexibility. Wiccans may need to adapt their spiritual routines to accommodate their other responsibilities, finding ways to integrate their beliefs into their schedules.

Social considerations also come into play when balancing Wiccan beliefs with other aspects of life. Not all individuals know or accept Wicca, and some may hold misconceptions or biases about the religion. Wiccans may choose to be discreet about their beliefs in specific social or professional settings to avoid potential discrimination or prejudice. This discretion can be a protective measure, but it can also create a sense of isolation or the feeling of living a double life, where one's spiritual beliefs remain hidden.

Additionally, the commercialization and trivialization of Wiccan practices in popular culture can pose challenges for practitioners who strive to maintain the authenticity and sacredness of their beliefs. The proliferation of mass-produced Wiccan items and the misrepresentation of the tradition in media can lead to frustration or disillusionment among Wiccans who seek to uphold the integrity of their spiritual practices.

Despite these challenges, finding balance between Wiccan beliefs and other aspects of life offers numerous benefits. Integrating spiritual practices into daily routines can lead to a greater sense of purpose, inner peace, and personal growth. Wiccans often find that their beliefs provide them with guidance, support, and resilience in facing life's challenges. The mindfulness and intentionality cultivated through Wiccan practices can lead to a deeper appreciation of the present moment and a more profound connection to the natural world.

Moreover, finding balance between Wiccan beliefs and other life aspects fosters authenticity and congruence. Wiccans who are true to their beliefs in all areas of life often report feeling more aligned with their values and a greater sense of harmony. This authenticity can also positively impact relationships, as it encourages open and honest communication with loved ones about one's spiritual beliefs.

In conclusion, balancing Wiccan beliefs with other aspects of life is a complex and ongoing endeavor that requires mindfulness, intentionality, and adaptability. Wiccans strive to integrate their spiritual practices into daily routines, infusing everyday activities with intention and meaning. While challenges related to time management, social considerations, and commercialization exist, the benefits of finding balance are profound, including a greater sense of authenticity, personal growth, and alignment with one's values. Ultimately, balancing Wiccan beliefs with everyday life is deeply personal and transformative, allowing practitioners to walk their spiritual path with grace and resilience.

Finding Fulfillment through the Craft

Wicca, often called "the Craft," is more than just a spiritual path; it is a source of profound fulfillment for many of its practitioners. Rooted in pagan and witchcraft traditions, Wicca offers a unique blend of spirituality, magic, and reverence for nature that resonates with those who seek a deeper connection to themselves and the world around them. In this section, we will explore how Wicca brings fulfillment to those who embrace it, including the sense of empowerment, personal growth, community, and the deep connection to the natural world that it fosters.

One of the most transformative aspects of Wicca is the sense of empowerment it offers to its practitioners. Wiccans often describe a feeling of taking control of their lives and their destinies through the Craft. This empowerment is rooted in the belief that individuals can shape their reality, influence the outcomes of their actions, and connect with the divine within themselves. Through rituals, spells, and magical workings, Wiccans harness their inner power and channel it to manifest their intentions. This sense of personal agency and empowerment can lead to a profound shift in how practitioners perceive themselves and their place in the world.

Personal growth is another key source of fulfillment in Wicca. The spiritual journey of a Wiccan is characterized by continuous self-discovery and transformation. Wiccans gain a deeper understanding of themselves and their motivations through meditation, reflection, and introspection. They confront their fears, insecurities, and limiting beliefs, working to overcome them and become more authentic versions of themselves. This process of self-improvement and growth is a fundamental aspect of the Craft and is often seen as a lifelong journey of becoming the best possible self.

Community plays a crucial role in the fulfillment that Wicca offers. Many Wiccans find a sense of belonging and support within the Wiccan community through covens, study groups, or online communities. These connections provide a space for individuals to share their experiences, learn from one another, and celebrate their spirituality together. The sense of community fosters a feeling of acceptance and validation, reducing feelings of isolation that some practitioners may experience in mainstream society. In addition, it allows Wiccans to collectively engage in rituals and celebrations, deepening their connection to the Craft and their fellow practitioners.

The deep connection to the natural world is a central source of fulfillment for many Wiccans. Nature is revered as sacred, and the moon's cycles, seasons, and elements hold profound spiritual significance. Wiccans often spend time outdoors in the wilderness, a garden, or a city park to connect with the natural world and draw inspiration from it. Observing the changing of the seasons, the phases of the moon, and the earth's rhythms becomes a spiritual practice in itself, reinforcing the sense of harmony and interconnectedness with the environment. Additionally, the Craft provides a framework for ethical living that contributes to the sense of fulfillment. The Wiccan Rede states, "An it harm none, do what ye will," guides practitioners in their ethical decision-making. This guideline promotes responsible and ethical behavior, encouraging practitioners to consider the potential consequences of their actions on themselves, others, and the environment. Living in alignment with these ethical principles contributes to a sense of moral integrity and fulfillment, as practitioners feel that they are making choices that are not only spiritually meaningful but also ethically sound.

While Wicca offers profound fulfillment to those who practice it, it is not without its challenges. Wiccans may face misconceptions, prejudices, or misunderstandings about their beliefs, which can create tension or discomfort in social or professional settings. Additionally, finding a balance between Wiccan practices and the demands of everyday life can be challenging, as practitioners strive to integrate their spirituality into their daily routines.

In conclusion, Wicca, or "the Craft," offers a unique and profoundly fulfilling spiritual path that empowers individuals, fosters personal growth, builds a sense of community, and promotes a deep connection to the natural world. The sense of empowerment, personal agency, and the continuous process of self-discovery and growth are sources of profound fulfillment for Wiccans. The sense of belonging within the Wiccan community and the reverence for the natural world further enhance this fulfillment. Despite the challenges and misconceptions that Wiccans may encounter, the Craft continues to offer a rich and rewarding spiritual journey for those who embrace it, providing a sense of purpose, meaning, and deep connection to the world around them.

CONCLUSION

In "Wiccan Philosophy and Ethics: Wiccan Wisdom-Exploring the Philosophy and Ethics of the Craft," we have embarked on a journey into Wicca's profound and spiritually enriching world. Throughout this e-book, we have explored the fundamental principles, beliefs, and practices that underpin Wiccan philosophy and ethics. From the historical roots of Wicca to the significance of the Wiccan Rede and the Threefold Law, we have delved into the core tenets that guide Wiccans on their spiritual paths.

We have also explored the essential role of the elements, the tools of the craft, and the significance of rituals and celebrations in Wiccan practice. Through these explorations, we have uncovered the interconnectedness of all life, the reverence for nature, and the importance of balance, responsibility, and ethical consideration in every magickal working.

As we conclude our journey, we are left with a deep appreciation for Wicca's wisdom and spirituality. It is a path that encourages self-discovery, personal growth, and a harmonious connection with the divine and the natural world. The philosophy and ethics of Wicca, rooted in the belief of "Harm None" and the principle of balance, serve as guiding lights for practitioners to navigate their lives with mindfulness and reverence.

In the ever-evolving landscape of spirituality, Wicca is a vibrant and inclusive tradition that celebrates diversity, empowerment, and the sacredness of all existence. As we close the pages of this ebook, may the wisdom and ethics of the Craft continue to inspire and guide us on our own spiritual journeys, fostering a deep and abiding connection with the divine, the elements, and the intricate tapestry of life.

Thank you for buying and reading/ listening to our book. If you found this book useful/ helpful please take a few minutes and leave a review on the platform where you purchased our book. Your feedback matters greatly to us.